KNOWING THE
LORD JESUS CHRIST
THROUGH SUFFERING AND PAIN
WAS A HARD THING TO BEAR

MELROE NEWTON

authorHOUSE

AuthorHouse™
1663 Liberty Drive
Bloomington, IN 47403
www.authorhouse.com
Phone: 1 (800) 839-8640

Published by AuthorHouse 07/30/2019

ISBN: 978-1-5462-4510-0 (sc)
ISBN: 978-1-5462-4508-7 (hc)
ISBN: 978-1-5462-4509-4 (e)

Library of Congress Control Number: 2018906519

Print information available on the last page.

Any people depicted in stock imagery provided by Getty Images are models, and such images are being used for illustrative purposes only. Certain stock imagery © Getty Images.

This book is printed on acid-free paper.

Because of the dynamic nature of the Internet, any web addresses or links contained in this book may have changed since publication and may no longer be valid. The views expressed in this work are solely those of the author and do not necessarily reflect the views of the publisher, and the publisher hereby disclaims any responsibility for them.

Scripture taken from The Holy Bible, King James Version. Public Domain

Contents

Introduction and Acknowledgment ix

Chapter 1   To Know Jesus! You Have To Find Him 1

Chapter 2   Getting To Know More About The Church. 5

Chapter 3   Resposibility That I Faces 7

Chapter 4   Persecution I Have Gone Through 10

Chapter 5   New Experience I Had During My Training. 17

Chapter 6   Problems Of Which I Could Not Understand 22

Chapter 7   Experience I Had With God's Help!. 39

Chapter 8   Accepting God's Calling 41

Chapter 9   When I Came To The U.S.A, I Have New
             Experience, As If I Was In School. 45

Chapter 10   Experience I Had Before I Was Baptized .48

Chapter 11   Making My Own Decision Through God. 52

Chapter 12   There Is A Lot Of Different Things Jesus Is Aginst 53

Chapter 13   Knowing Jesus Through Your Love. 55

Chapter 14   God Can Do Things For You, At The Right Time! And The Right Place! 59

Chapter 15   The Ten Commandments Is A Law That
             God Ask Us To Follow In The Bible. 60

Chapter 16   The Angel Of The Lord Came To Me In God Mircles Work 62

Chapter 17   Important Experience That I Would Like To Shere. 64

Chapter 18   Fighting Against God Servants 65

Chapter 19   Showing Love To All People! And Honouring Mother's, And
             Father's, Through Jesus Love. 66

Chapter 20   Trial And Tribulation! After Accepting
The Lord As My Personal Savior From Sin! 68

Chapter 21   Discovering How Great God Can Be 70

Chapter 22   When You Know Jesus And Love Him!
You Will Know How Much You Can Have Faith In Him? 72

Chapter 23   Overcoming Strugelling Times Through God's Love. 73

Chapter 24   Jesus Is The Savior! He Will Lead You, If You Let Him In 74

Chapter 25   Danger That Is Unberable And Only The Lord Could Help! 76

Chapter 26   "Be Ready!" For The Lord Jesus Is Saying To Us, We Need To Be Ready
For The Coming Of Our Lord And Savior Jesus Christ! 77

Chapter 27   Massage From God! 78

Chapter 28   Satan Fighting Against God Servants! 79

Chapter 29   Crusified With Out Being Nailed To The Cross! 80

Chapter 30   Jesus Is The Key To All The Hearts That Need To Be Open! 84

Chapter 31   Jesus Is The Key To All The Hearts That Need To Be Open! 87

Chapter 32   Beliving In Jesus Servants Is Very Important 89

Chapter 33   Beliving In God Law! 91

Chapter 34   Being On Time To Go To Heaven! 93

Chapter 35   Jesus Was Crusified On The Cross! Why
Did He Not Walk Away From The Wickeds 95

Chapter 36   Being Lock Away As Daniel In The Lion Den! God Was The Only Savior 96

Chapter 37   When You Come To Know Jesus And Love Him 98

Chapter 38   Jesus Was Crusified On The Cross! Why
Did He Not Walk Away From The Wickeds! 99

Chapter 39   Being Lock Away As Daniel In The Lion Den! God Was The Only Savior 101

Chapter 40   When You Come To Know Jesus And Love Him! 103

Chapter 41   I Have Seen The Power Of God, And Prove His Strength. 104

Chapter 42   There Is Rules In God's House 106

Chapter 43   When Jesus Get's Ready? You Have To Be Ready! 108

Chapter 44   Trying To Serve The Lord, And Others Fighting Aginst You! 109

Chapter 45   Knowing The Lord, And Remembering When The Struggle Is Over,
And God Shine The Light Of Delevereance Over You, With Joy And
Happeness! 111

Chapter 46   When I Come To Know The Lord, And
              See The Work He Want Me To Do!....................................112

Chapter 47   To Know The Lord Is Not On Easy Thing To Do!.......................114

Chapter 48   Jesus Is Love!..116

Chapter 49   Jesus Is Alive! I Have Proved Him, In Ways That Is Amazing...........118

Chapter 50   Disadvantages, That Happen To God Servants Through Learing To
              Know Jesus Our Lord And Savior!....................................120

Chapter 51   Satan Used Others To Take All I Had! Yet
              Jesus Let Me See Heaven Even Clearer!..............................122

Chapter 52   Looking To Jesus At All Times, Even Before Disappointment Comes!.....124

Chapter 53   Jesus Save, No Matter How Hopeless It May Seems! He Can Save You....126

Chapter 54   The Good Samaritam Comes To My Help!...............................128

Chapter 55   The Healing Power Of God, I Have Experience! God Great And
              Marvelous Work Through Working In The Nurcing Care!................130

Chapter 56   Jesus Is The Greatest Helper Of All! He Loves You, And Want's
              You To Put Your Trust In Him!......................................131

Chapter 57   To Know Jesus You Have To Love Him! To Know Yourself You Have
              To Be Taught From A Child..133

Chapter 58   The Healing Power Of God Is A Gift From God!.......................136

Chapter 59   God Holy Servants Is Every Were!...................................138

Chapter 60   Over Coming Power Is Real!...139

Chapter 61   To Know The Lord Before Saying Yes To Him Is Very Important!.........142

Chapter 62   Jesus Is True, Honest, Loving, And Sure Savior, When You Come
              To Know Him, You Will Never Want's To Leave Him!...................144

Chapter 63   To Learn Is Very Important In The Sight Of God And Man! In God's Eye
              You Have To Learn Of Him. In The Eyes Of Man You Have To Learn
              The Eartly Things Of Life..146

Chapter 64   When You Become Inspired In The Lord And Savior Jesus Christ!.......148

Chapter 65   The Chousen One, Which Sent From God! Our Father In Heaven!.........149

Chapter 66   God Work Need To Have Honest People, Care Giving People, Loving
              People, And Heard Working People To Save Souls For His Kingdom!.....151

Chapter 67   Working For A Honest Living! Jesus Said!
              We Should Live By The Sweet Of Our Brow............................153

Chapter 68   Discovering The Plan Of Salvation! And
              Of To Return Back To The World Of Sin!.............................155

Chapter 69   The Savior Is At Your Door! Let Him In! He Cares For You Always! 157

Chapter 70   I Am Here Lord! I Overcome The Stream
              And The Vallies I Come From For And Near. 160

Chapter 71   When We See The Signs Of Our Lord And Savior Coming, We Should
              Be Clouser Drown To Him, Not Runing Away From Him!. 161

Chapter 72   When A Savior Knocks At Your Door, Do You Know It's The Savior?. 163

Chapter 73   Jesus Save!. 166

Chapter 74   When We See The Signs Of Our Lord And
              Savior, We Should Be Clouser Drowning To Him!. .171

Chapter 75   When A Child Is Born From Her Mother's Whome!. 178

INTRODUCTION AND ACKNOWLEDGMENT

I have no writing staff or team of researchers who provide me with historical and illustrative material or serve as my advisories for my book. Every word comes from my brain and from the Holy Spirit, and from the Holy words of God, and also from unproductive days when everything seems hopeless, and periodic moments when inspiration and incite flows, I don't even use a word processor. I depend on the loving God of heaven and earth to lead my brain and my heart in writing this book. He is all loving and caring God, and a God of inspiration

CHAPTER 1

TO KNOW JESUS! YOU HAVE TO FIND HIM

I was brought up, and born again in the Seventh – day – Adventist Church, my mother and fathers were a member there. They taught me all about the subject of God, and how to love and worship him. Which was exceptionally good? I acknowledge their teaching, and grew to love God. I was married extremely young, at the age of 17 years old. I did not like my early marriage. I always want to continually in getting a carrier, and in addition I always desire to know what happening in the world. I was married to a man that was not an Adventist man. I always constantly study my Bible, of which I did not imagine it could tell me all I need to know.

I always constantly devoted to be around in the region of people who have a discussion regarding the government and politics. It's also impossible knowing other things about the world without God. During my life experience I always have difficult times. God was always there for me. I always thank God Throughout my existence understanding that he granted to me, I believe God have me for a special reason. When I have encompassed a problem and turn to in the direction of Jesus I always find piece and comfort in him. I always love and fare him. During the time of my marriage, I have seen lots of difficult times. I start having children very fast. I always because that not what my life first. God always take care of them. My husband always has a job. He did his best to take care of his children, which I was very grateful. In 1977 my husband had has on accident which he approximately dies. I cry until I nearly past out, and would have to go in the direction to the hospital. I could remember asking my father to get me a drink. He bought me the drink, and I drink it. I went home from the hospital. I send and bought another drink, and drink again for a second time. I was thinking that it could help the pain I was feeling inside of me. It did not help me I got sick. I was so unfilled in side. All I was doing was crying and asking them to take me to the hospital. No one takes me in the direction of the hospital. I went to sleep, as soon as I wake up the next morning, I lay right and my bed and I prayed and place my husband before God. My prayer was answer, God told me he would not die. I went to the hospital to see him the other day, and he was move to a privet hospital, where he was taken care of, and he got better and come home. I take care of him until he was well again, but he was unable to go back to work, because of the burn on his hands. I decided to travel in order to get a Job to help my family. I got a job, and was working minimum wage. I could not pay all my bills from that wage. I start looking for another job. I got another Job, working from 4:30 pm in the after noon, until 12:30am at nights, doing assembling electronic parts. I was working 6am until 12:30 at nights. I save and I bought a used car. I worked two jobs for all most one year. I was so tired I could not awake up one morning to go to work. I could just reach for the phone and call my boss and quit my first job. After a few months with the other job, they went out of business. I was living on my own and out of a job for two weeks. love to read, at the same time as well be devoted in the direction of reading love stories from different books; watches love stories on T.V. also in addition license to the radio means of communication. Of which help me to learn a lot about the direction of gaining knowledge of an assortment in relation, in the direction of things of the world. I recognize what was happening around me in the region of the world, it was very extremely important. My mother always constantly tells me the Bible have contain ever thing that obsession to facilitate you need in the direction you to know. Which I presume is true. When I start to in the direction of having a family of my own, I trained my children all about school, Church education and going to house of worship. I explain clearly about school, because without a education they will have a hard time in life, for the reason that I believed having a carrier is very important when they grew up. As a result when they grew up they can take care of themselves. Church House of worship was also exceptionally important; for the reason they will know more about God, it's one of my coworker calls me and told me she saw a job in the news paper, and we should go and fill on application. I went and we got the job. I had another experience which I could not understand; it was the voice of God! I had a vision which Jesus shown his him self to me in thy sky with two men beside him; he had a crown on his head. Yet I did not accept I went to London in 1980 after the death of my father, to visit my family. Some of the pain goes away, as soon as I see my family, and how nicely they treated me. I spend tree months and went back to Jamaica to see my husband and children. Life was not easy; I always wanted to come to in the direction of America and work in assistance to my children. God help me and I got a visa. Therefore I came to the U.S.A. 15th December1980. I went to New York and a friend comes and gets me at the air port. I stayed with her for two weeks; I work one week with a family, taking care of their baby. I did not like to live in New York, because of this reason, it was too freezing cold and crowded. My brother and his wife was living in Florida, I called him and he told me to come to Florida. I borrow some money from my girl friend and purchase a ticket and came to Florida. When I came to Florida! I loved it very much, I stayed with my brother and his wife, and I started looking for a job. I got a job from a friend of my brother, in a factory, trimming swim suit. I needed another job, because I could not manage my bills, my friend saw a job in the paper, as on electronic tester. We booth went for the interview. I was told to come back and see the boss in the afternoon. I went back and see the boss and I got the job. I work with that company for 4 years. I was happy making money, and taking care of my self and family. I change my car for a new car, because it was giving me a lot of problems. During the time on the job, I start seeing things I could not understand. I was freighted and scared. I cry some times. I told my boss a few things. And my work mate who I work with in the test room. I even see things about my family and call my family in London and told them things. They did not believe. I start having lots of problems, of which I could not understand. I always prayed. Some times, I would write my prayer because I could not speak. Sometimes I suffer a lot of disadvantage where I was living. I was not making enough money to take care of my family, pay for my car and get a place of my own. During the time I was suffering I was told that I was going to have a little girl baby, I did not take it into consideration, because of difficult; I was divorce from my husband. So I did not worry about it; I woke up one morning, and my next doors neighbored ask me to go to the park with her. I taught about it and I said yes. I drove her to snider park in Hollywood, where they had a bond playing. A young man came to me and was speaking to me. We communicate for a while, and then I leave and go some were else. After a few minutes he came back to me. He asks me for my phone number I gave it to him, one week later he called me. We started to communicate, until we developed a relationship. After we start being friendly, he asks me to be his lady. I said yes, but I could not live with you without being married. He wanted to come and live with me where I was living. I never lived with a man with out being married. I was scared and I know it was not right. I was very lonely so we keep seeing each other. It really happen I got pregnant I was very happy about it, I feel like it was my first child. I really have a little girl. I love her very much. I know that was God's work, because during my pregnancy I learn a lot. All that I start to learn was very surprising. I have a much harder time, because I leave my job. And her father was not very attentive to us. I take her to church and have her bless by the pastor of the church. It takes me a while to see what Jesus want me to do, because my life was in the wrong way. I decided that I was going to start going back to church. I went to church one Sabbath with a church sister and her husband. I sat and was very attentive to the service. There were some things I like, and some things I did not like. After the service I went home. I know right there and then some thing were wrong. I began to pray always. I would pray many times a day. When I go back I would look for changes. And I see changes. God answer prayers.

For the interview, I was told to come back and see the boss in the afternoon. I went back and see the boss and I get the job. I work with that company for 4 years. I was happy making money, and taking care of my self and family. I change my car for a new car, for the reason that it was giving me a lot of problems. During the time on the job, I start seeing things I could not understand. I was frightened. I cry some times! I told my boss a few things, and my work friend who I work with in the test room. I was determined to go back to the house of worship. I went to the house of worship one Sabbath with a church sister and her husband. I sit and was very attentive to the service. There were some things I like to here, and some things I did not like to here. After the service I went home! I know right there and then some thing were not right in God's house. I began to pray always. I would pray many times a day. When I go back I would look for changes. And I see changes. God answer prayers.

CHAPTER 2

GETTING TO KNOW MORE ABOUT THE CHURCH

I went back another Sabbath and I did sat and was attentive again. I came to realize that there was work for me to do for the Lord. I did not say a word to any one. When the minister called for people to accept the Lord as there personal savior from sin, I go straight to Jesus in tears. That was all I could do to help with Jesus work, at that time. I did not have money, I did not have clothes, but I put my self before the Lord, because I know there should be no failure in Jesus. I was having a lot of problem for the past 10 years. I lost my car, I lost my job. Because I was unable to work after I have my daughter. I was told that I have to do what God want me to do. After being baptize and began to read God words again carefully, I came to realize it is good, for some one to take advice from others, my mother always told me to follow God's words, if I was following at all times, my burden would not be so heavy. After I decided to travel to the U.S.A MY plans were to return back to Jamaica in one year, to see my children and try to bring them to the U.S.A. I start having problem; I realize that I could not go back until I do what God wants me to do. I wrote to my husband and ask him to come and joined me here in America, for a few weeks. He wrote back and refuses to come. We always have problems of our own, but I was still trying to keep the marriage going. I realize that all I was going through was in the Bible. I understand what has happened to me. And what God wants me to do. I suffer a lot to know Jesus was the true and living God. But I think it was for a good reason. I am now trying to do my best to follow his calling. My understanding becomes very clear. Thank God for knowledge. I have gone through difficult times before I know that Jesus was the only answer.

My prayer always answered. It was nice finding Jesus and I am still going to church. It's not easy to be there but because I know I make my decision to serve him until he comes, I know when I am with the Lord, I can not turn back. I waited a very long time to prove Jesus words. The reason I said it not easy to be there, is because I feel like when I was in the world of sin. I think its hurt even more, when I found out it's not much different from being with some of the people in the world. But because I know the true God of heaven can change any thing that is not right. I take it as a great responsibility to do what every God would like me to do. Some times it so heard on me, I feel like leaving many times. But I know I could not do so because he save me through ruff times and give me the opportunity to find him, so I know this is the work he wants me to do. I know that all I have to do is keep his law and trust in him and pray until ever one can see me clearly, and know I am sent from God as a servant.

CHAPTER 3

RESPOSIBILITY THAT I FACES

When I realize the great responsibility I face through out the world. I lay my entire burden on Jesus. I have to pray always. I began to have strong faith in God. I love him more. I do not worry about my problem any more. I just try to solve them. All I have to do was to keep my faith strong in Jesus, and face the facts of life. I do not like to remember the things I have gone through. I want to do the work God want me to do, and do it well. I always have strong faith in God, so I know I have to hold on to my faith in God. I know that God is reel, because I have tried other things, to find comfort and I could not find it. Because that other means was not in me. I have try going to parties of which I could not found that true love that I found with the Lord. When I go to God in prayer, I found joy, love, and happiness all over my heart. So I know I have made the right choice. I could remember there was a song that said there is two ways, you got to make your choice. I am happy every God give me the understanding to make the right choice, I would like every one that read this book to take it as an advice from Mel roe N. Ellis, and try to make the right choice, and chouse to know Jesus. Sometimes I try very hard to keep my marriage because of my kids. I know right away that it was not going to work for us any more. But because I have seeing the important of being here, I had to stay. I have been away from them for 12 years, December 15th 1992. Prayer helps me to do this on my own. I am still struggling, but because I found Jesus I know it was for all the good reason. So I give God thanks for the healing Power that he has given to me. Jesus is wonderful when you find him, and follow his laws. It's not on easy law to keep, but if you trust in him and have faith in him, you will love him and never want to leave him. Jesus love is very humble, loving, kind hearted, and pure. He will keep you, and care for you, if you give your heart to him. I would like to help every one to know him, because I have gone through it all to know Jesus. It was not easy but its turn out to be a joyful end. I am looking forward for a new life now, of which I do hope to be with Jesus. When you seek Jesus first, he promises that he will give you all things that you need.

We have to learn to trust him with all your heart, to have that promise be fulfills. Jesus loves us all no matter how difficult our problems are. Jesus said we should come just as we are, and he will add all things to your lives. I always say I could not go to church because I do not have things to wear. I put those saying out of my mind and I start going as I am. And Jesus really helps me to understand him and love him more. I know he will do the same for you too. I come to know him and I start working for Jesus. I went to church one Sabbath morning; I was so tired that I could only stay until the mid day service was over. I went home and could not return to the rest of the day's service. I have been face with many different works; I have to have a clear mind, and strength to make the right choice. I have to depend on Jesus. He always sends help in many different ways. Before I got baptize my work was very difficult to deal with, but after finding Jesus in the right way he inspired me in a mighty way. Dealing with having to be encounter in the midst of difficult times, despite the fact that I was training to perform my work, was extremely hard for me to accomplish. I recognize it was extremely important for me to know Jesus, and able to be capable toward perform his work. I love working with people who desire in the direction of learning and would like to understand Jesus. terminology. Working with people is wonderful.

I could remember when I start to learn to drive in Jamaica, the instructor take me in the busy street streets of Spanish town, of which I learn to drive quickly, I gain knowledge of driving in three days. I was driving on the high ways in three days. After coming to America and observe how busy the streets were. I perceive how important it was for me to do so. God know what he was doing. I had to leave to be in America shortly after I learn to drive and got my driver license. The roads were full actively. I have managed extremely well for a few years driving my self to work, until I have to give it all up for a period of time, and find Jesus. God always have his servants trained in many different ways. Now I came too realized with the intention that God has a special job work designed for me to. perform. I will do it with self-control and perform it through Jesus help. Jesus knows I can do his will, because for the reason that he has sought me and discover me. At the times I went to London I acquire a vision, telling how I was preaching inside a Church. And I did not take it serious; I now come to know that it was a very especially important vision. I also have another vision of the Ten Commandments written in the sky, and there were three men beside each other. There was one man in the middle with a crown on top of his head, and two others on each side. I believe he was pointing out the commands and the risen savior. I was disappearing one night into my sleep, and I have another vision I heard a voice, telling me I should wake up and read Psalm 71. It was amazing to see the things God has put me through to know him. I have gone through a lot to know Jesus. Thank God I accept the final calling I have found the true and living God.

CHAPTER 4
PERSECUTION I HAVE GONE THROUGH

Subsequent to loosing my Job and car I start having problem with paying my rent, and I have to move from one place to another. My daughter and I have gone through a very great deal to know that I must perform God will. I am still at the moment going through difficult time. However I am praying and trusting the excellent Lord and his Holy Spirit that they will have me doing his will very soon. I discern that his strength of character will take care of my problems. To do my work, that I know is very important to me. I have strength from God. I have to work with in the midst of people who are honest, and heard working, and loving. I recognize that I cannot do it on my own; to accomplish Jesus work I have to work with others. I came to realize that my entire walk of life with God is depending upon our Lord and savior Jesus Christ. To inspired me, to lead me with helping ever one to walk in the foot step, with of Jesus words and have them follow Jesus. Following Jesus principles I have been through stage where I was push to live in this world dirty, stupid, lazy unintelligent, and with out friends, even not to speak truth. Jesus took me out of all those problems, so I know; therefore I recognize he will execute the identical thing for any one who need to know Jesus help. When I decided to have my baby Kimberly, I recognize it was only God the supernatural being could give permission to me as a result I could make that decision. I am very happy, extremely cheerful to know I did not have her for a worst man. I could be acquainted with a most horrible gentleman than her father. I was attentive to my work so much, I know a man from God had to capture my heart and help me. After all that I have gone through. I am praying that if I should have to do it again, Jesus would give me the strength to make the right decision. With out Jesus assistant it's really hard for me. I know what ever he want to be done has to be done. Therefore I have to depend on Jesus always. I would like every one trying to be acquainted with Jesus for them- selves should read his words and follow them and listen to the Angels with the still small voice. The equipment I did used to know Jesus first was, I love Jesus with all my heart. If you read his words with understanding you will grew to love him. When you care about Jesus, and you put ever effort in finding him, he will reveille him self to you, and help you to know him and love him. He cares about every one that cares for him 1 Peter 5: 7, it tells you how much he cares! Costing all your care upon him; for he careth for you. If you cost all your problems on him, he will lead you always. I come to prove him for my self. And I know if you try he will do the same for you. To know Jesus! Sometimes you have to go through different trial and tribulation. After coming to know Jesus, you will love him and keep trying to do what ever is right to help you to keep your faith in him. And go on living in Jesus name. Jesus calling is very sure calling. When he needs you he will not leave you. Sometimes it seems hopeless, but as the song writer says never give up, only trust in the Lord, and take hold. Jesus is the answer to any problems. He will not turn you away, he will not leave you, and he will never fail you. He always loves you no matter how hope less it may seem. I am saying these important words about him because I come to know him and prove him, so I know him his sure God of heaven and earth. He loves me and saves me, and I know he will save you too. Obey his words and follow him, and he will never fail you. Jesus is coming soon! I do hope when a Jesus come every one will be ready to see him. I can see it will be a glorious time. We all want to see him! We should start serving Jesus and follow his words carefully.

There is one thing in my life that I have experience, that I would like all parents to pay carefully attention to when they start having a family. You should show all your children the same love, which is God's love! Remember when I start having a family I always try to dress them all alike just to show them that I love them all with one love. There is many different ways in which I always do thing for them to show them that I love them all.

If you read Jesus words with understanding you will grow to love him. When you think about Jesus, and you put increasingly endeavor into finding him, Jesus will reveille his character to you, and be of assistance to you knowing him and loving him. Jesus care about every one that care for him 1 Peter 5: 7, it tells you how much he cares if you cost all your problems on him. I come to prove him for my self. And I know if you make an effort, Jesus will assist you to prove him for your self also. To know Jesus! Sometimes you have to pass through different trial and tribulation. Subsequent to coming to know Jesus, you will love him and maintain irritating in the direction of perform what ever is necessary to be of assistance to maintain faithfulness in him.

And go on living in Jesus name. Jesus calling is very definite mission. Once he desires you to do his will, Jesus will not disappear from you. Occasionally it seems unpromising, nevertheless since the song author say never give up, only trust in the Lord, and take hold. Jesus is the answer toward any tribulations! He will not turn you away, Jesus will not leave you, and he will by no means fail you. He always loves you, even when the rejection seems hopeless. I am saying these important words about him for the reason that I come to discern him and prove him to be mighty father of all, so I recognize Jesus to be definite God of heaven and earth. He loves me and saves me, and I identify that he will save you as well. Obey his words and follow them, and he will on no account fail you. Jesus is coming soon! I look forward at what time Jesus approaches every individual will be equipped to see him. I can perceive it will be a glorious time. We all want to see him! We should establish serving Jesus and follow his words carefully.

I came to realize how important it was to do so. I thank God for his inspiration. You should never give up, learn to pray to Jesus always, ask him for your need, he will here your prayer and answer while you are true to him. Some times it seems like what you ask for is impossible. Just have faith in God and believed that he will help you, he may seem slow, but he is a sure God. Matthew 21: 21, 22, tell you that, Verily I say unto you, if you have faith and doubt not, ye shall not only do this which is done to the fig tree, but also if ye shall say unto the mountain, Be thou removed and be thou cost into the sea; it shall be done. And all things, what-so-ever he asks in prayer, believing, ye shall receive. He or she should ask in prayer ye shall receive. Jesus is our savior, he will never leave you. You should try to know him and trust him always. It's so wonderful when you have Jesus; you feel his wonderful love always. It's a joyful feeling in you that you would never want to loose. Trusting him is the first thing to do, to start having his wonderful love. Jesus cares for every one who cares for him. When Jesus is in you, there is nothing you can do wrong. Before I came to know Jesus I have done things that I was told to do and I still did not know it was the son of God was leading me. Jesus is a sweet savior! I would like every one to come to know him, and follow him. Some times we have to suffer to know Jesus. But we should learn to trust him and love him, so he can always be in your hearts. When you have to give up things for Jesus you will do it if you really love him. Taking advice from others some times is very good. It's hard to give up on things that you really need, such as money, every one need money, but when it do not comes from good order it is bad for you. When you are part taker of Jesus suffering, you will gain strength from Jesus. Straight is the way of the Lord. Accepting the Lord as your savior, and learn to love him and trust him always. And get baptize in Jesus name, when you need strength and authority from God you have to know him, trust him, and obey his words. When you obey his rules, you need not worry. He will be always there for you through his words and prayer. Jesus said! We must first love him and follow his foot step. And love others as we love our selves. As we learn to do what he asks, he will always help you. Sometimes you will experience difficult times when you are learning to obey his rules. You should never give up. Learn to pray to Jesus always, ask him for what you need. With out we serve Jesus we will not have that happiness he promises us. I know every one of us would love to be running to him when he comes. So we have to ask him through prayer to help us to know him and love him. Jesus coming is sure; we all need to be sure we are ready. When we love Jesus and serve him, he will have thing work out for us. It will be amazing to know Jesus will do such wonderful things for us. Just give him a chance in your life, he desires to help you. Jesus said! If we can be like a little child he is willing to help us to enter into his kingdom. Jesus has his messenger come to you in many different ways. So in reading this book you will find that this is one way in which God reach out to his people, through his servants. Come to Jesus now! We are in the end of time. He loves you very much, and desires you to be saving in his kingdom. When I had the vision at the age of 18 years of age, about the Ten Commandments, I also see on the sky, there was three men in the sky, the one in the middle had a crown on his head. After thinking about the vision, and see what I am going through at the age of 43. I could see clearly that the vision was telling me about Jesus Christ and the crucifixion of Jesus and his resurrection. He was on the cross with two thieves. And he raises and was crown as Lord of the world.

There is one thing in my life that I have experience, is that I would like each and every parent to carefully attended to ever one of their children, at what time they establish having a family of there own. They ought to show each and every one of their children the same love, which is God's love! I can remember as soon as I begin having a family I always try to dress them all similarly, just to demonstrate to them that I love every single one with one love. There are many different ways in which at all times I do thing for them, to illustrate to them, and giving them the understanding that I love them all.

I did not understand that God was showing me that I would be facing with a symbol of his crucifixion. I came to experience it at the age of 43 years. I have rented a room in a house, where I can tell you that is only the son of God could take me out. God let me see every thing I was facing. And then he let me remember the vision I had at 18 years of age. After coming to know Jesus as my personal savior from sin, and think of the trial and tribulation I have gone through, to know he was always with me. And he was the one who take me through. I love him even more. And after studding his Holy Bible and see what God servants had gone through. I have a joy in my heart that bubbles over. I am happy to know what he can do to save souls. Looking at Job suffering and see what he has gone through, and yet he loves God even more and has faith in Jesus. Job: 31 tell you about his commitment and sentence to God. I would like every one to come to know Jesus as I do and have faith in God always. He is a wonderful and caring God. Jesus through his father can salve any problems. So all we have to do is to love him and try to serve him. Luke 7: 16-21 Tell you haw great Jesus is. And there cane a fear on all: and glorified God saying, that a great Prophet is risen up among us; and that God hath visited his people. And this rumour of him went forth throughout the entire region round about. And the disciples sent them to Jesus, saying, Art thou he that should come? Or look we for another? When the men were come unto him they said, John Baptist hath sent us unto thee, saying, Art thou he that should come? Or look for another? And in the same hour he cured many of their infirmities and plagues, and of evil spirits; and unto many that were blind he give sight. God can help you to over come all your infirmities and heal you from all fears and danger. So when you become a child of God, have faith in him! Never give up, he will help you, if you love and trust him. He is true and sure!

I come to realize how important it was to do so. I thank God for his inspiration. You should never give up, learn to pray to Jesus constantly, ask him for what you required, he will here your prayer and answer, at the same time, be true to him and sincere. Occasionally it seems like what you ask for is impossible. Just have faith in God and believed that he will be of assistance to you, he may seem slow, but he is a sure God. Matthew 21: 21, 22 tell you that if you have faith and douth not, whatsoever he asks, he or she should ask in prayer, believing; ye shall receive and he will receive. Jesus is our savior, his determination for us in this world, is that we serve him, and Jesus promises that he will never leave us. You should make an effort to know Jesus and trust him at all times. It's so wonderful when you have Jesus; you feel his wonderful love constantly in your heart. It's a joyful feeling inside you that you would never desire to loose. Trusting Jesus is the first thing to accomplish, toward start having his wonderful love. Jesus cares for every one who cares for him. When Jesus is inside you, there is nothing you can perform wrong. Before I came to know Jesus as my personal savior from sin, I have done things that I was told to execute, and yet I did not know it was the son of God that was leading me. Jesus is a sweet savior! I would like every one to come to know him, and follow him. Some times we have to suffer to know Jesus. But we should learn to trust him and love him; therefore he can constantly be in your hearts. Sometime you have to give up things to know Jesus; you will execute doing what you have to perform, if you really love him. Taking advice from others sometimes is very good. It's heard to give up on things you really need, such as money, every one needs money, but when it do not comes from good order it is bad for you. When you are part taker of Jesus suffering, you will gain strength from Jesus. Straight is the way of the Lord. Accepting the Lord as your savior, and learn to love him and trust him always. And get baptize in Jesus name, when you need strength and authority from God you have to know him, and trust him and obey his words. When you obey his rules, you need not worry. He will be always there for you through his words and prayer. Jesus said! We must first love him and follow his foot step. And love others as we love ourselves. At the same time as we learn to do what he asks, Jesus will constantly assist you. Sometimes you will experience difficult times when you are learning to obey his rules. You ought to never give up. Learn to pray to Jesus at all times, ask him for what you need. With out we serve Jesus we will not have that happiness he promises us. I know every one of us would love to be running to him when he comes. Therefore we have to ask him through prayer to help us to know him and love him. Jesus coming is sure; we all need to be sure we are ready. When we love Jesus and serve him, he will have difficulties taken away from us. It will be amazing to know Jesus will do such wonderful things for us. Just give him a chance in your life, he wants to help you. Jesus said! If we can be like a little child, he is willing to help us to enter into his kingdom. Jesus has his messenger come to you in many different ways. So in reading this book you will find that this is one way in which God reach out to his people, through his servants. Come to Jesus now! We are in the end of time. He loves you very much, and desires for you to be saving in his kingdom. When I had the vision at the age of 18 years of age, about the Ten Commandments, I also see on the sky, there was three men in the sky, the one in the middle had a crown on his head. After thinking about the vision, and see what I am going through at the age of 43. I could see clearly that the vision was telling me about Jesus Christ and the crucifixion of Jesus, and his resurrection. He was on the cross with two thieves. And he was raised on three day after his burial. Jesus is our savior; we need to serve him always.

CHAPTER 5

NEW EXPERIENCE I HAD DURING MY TRAINING

In august of 1992 we had on hurricane which hit Miami, and another state. There were a lot of people loose their homes, cars, and all that they had work for over the years. That's a heard thing for any one to deal with. I felt it very bad for them, because I have experience of loosing things too. So I did not understand that God was showing me that I would be facing with a symbol of his crucifixion. I came to experience it at the age of 43 years. I have rented a room in a house, where I can tell you that is only the son of God could take me out in the right order. God let me see every thing I was facing. And then he let me remember the vision I had at 18 years of age. After coming to know how heard it is. It helps me to get closer with Jesus Christ. I do hope every one will take these signs as a warning, and try to choose God as their personal savior from sin. I think of the trial and tribulation I have gone through, to know Jesus, and I love him better as I know him better, so that when these things happen, we will able to deal with problems like these, through Jesus love. Jesus will soon come! And we all need to be with him in his kingdom, there will be no more suffering, or hurricane to harm us. Jesus our savior will soon come; I said to my self, I know he will not let me be in danger. He promises to take me out of all danger. This is another experience I had; I was out of a Job at that time, and I was having problem paying my rent. I went to church on Sabbath morning. When I come home from church the land lady ask me if I got a place. I told her I did not have a place as yet. I was expecting a call from my Poster wife regarding a place, I went back to church, and spend the after noon at the meeting. I came home and waited until 9: pm and did not receive the call. So I keep praying in my heart that the good Lord will soon work out a way for me to get a place to live. I come to realize that I am a child of God, and these are some of the things that will test my faith with God. When I was about 18 years of age, I have my first vision, about the Ten Commandments. I keep it in my memory, but I did not exercise it as strong as I ought to. When I was 30 years of age I had my second vision of which I also kept in my brain. It was about preaching in a Church, and what I should drink for my health. I did try the health part of the vision. Not knowing it was so important for me to do as I was told, I keep praying for strength to do so. Matthew 7: 26 Tell's you that any one here my voice and do it not, shall be like the man that build his house upon a sand. Jesus voice can comes in many different ways. Therefore we should try to know him in the right way. He is sure, true and loving and you can trust him, he will never let you down. A Jesus said! You should not with drown your self from the world in order to escape from persecution; you should with your old heart loving him. Persecution will always come where every you are. All you need to do is to trust in Jesus Christ and pray always and ask Jesus to guide you through all things. When you have Jesus with you; you will always love every body, even when they are against you. And you will always want to help them too. To be a child of God you must go through trials and tribulation. I know people who have done me wrong and yet I love them all. With Jesus love you should not hate any one. That's one of the reason I know I am a follower of Jesus Christ. He will son to come, we must try to find him. I find him at the age of 41 years old, and I promise to give him the rest of my life on earth to serve him, and help others to know him. Now I have come to the time when I have to face the world and tell them about God wonderful work according to the Bible, I have to be ordained to speak to others in the sanctuary. I have to go into special prayer and care for my body. Jesus is the only answer for my work. Jesus is a Merciful savior. He can do great things. And he is patient with us. When you think of a mother who has conceived and bring forth a child in her whom for nine month isn't that a wonderful thing? I could remember when I start having my children, I always planning for them and saying how many children I would have, not knowing that God has plans for me. I even stop my self with a Doctor from having children. And God open my womb and gave me two more kids, and prove to me how great he is. I did not know from my mother that God has given me to my mother for a special gift. So God planed for me. Jesus can lead the way for all of us, if we only let him have a place in our hearts. No matter how heard it may seem. I love him even more when I come to know him, and know that he was the one who always keep me through all the bad times. I really want to shear the love of Jesus with others. I am praying that he will open every door for me, to tell others about Jesus, and how good he is to me. Gen.12: 1-3 Tell's me that when Jesus wants his Prophets to do his work, he will move you to a land where he will make your name great. Some times when you are with your own people It's seems so heard to tell the love of Jesus. So that is why Jesus will put you any were he can used you to do his work. Writing this book is one of my ways of telling others how wonderful Jesus can be to us. When a person get a brain from God! This is a special blessing. You should use it with special care. Using your brain to do the thing which is not right is a very wrong thing to do. We should always use it in the will of our Lord and savior Jesus Christ. And ask him to help you to do ever thing that you would like to do. Your brain is a very important part of your body. God should always be the leader of it. The responsibility of God work is a great one! God work is saving souls. Jesus dies on the cross to take away our sins. How can we as human beans not show love and honesty to one another? When a person of God's ability working to save souls and lives, they should be honest, that others can trust them, Jesus need honest, heard working people to do his work. Jesus work is a fundamental one; we should follow his words carefully. He suffers and dies so we can try to be holy as he is. He cares for us, and he wants us to care for others as well. My baby daughter came in this world at very critical time in my life. The way in witch she came was a very crucial way. I have to make that decision to have her in a way that hurt; I know that it would bring pain to my heart. But I had to have her because the child was needed in my work to help me over come the tribal ordeal. Satan was in the midst, and God need a special angel in my life to help me over come. I have over come, and the child has grown to be a woman. I give God thanks, to show me such great and mighty work. I want to continue to praise the soon coming king, until he comes. But I can not stand to see a child like that been hurt. All my children had been hurt because of the problems. The pains of children being hurt give me heart pain. I believe the good Lord will continue to help me to help her to be strong. And keep following the Lord words. I take her to the church of God hoping that she will be taught how to follow the word of God. It's not that easy as I taught, I am trying my best to show her the way through the Holy Bible. I do hope as she become a woman she will follow my words and the words of God. I am facing the same decision again, but because I come to know Jesus and what he stand for I will not make that decision on my own again. Jesus need an angel that he will use only to do his work, Jesus work has to do in the right way. So I am praying that he will guide me into truth, and the right person to make that decision with. I put my trust in God and I know he will take my angels through. I put them all in the hands of our Lord and savior Jesus Christ. He promises me that he will take care of them. I have seen his great and marvelous work; I know what he can do, so I put my trust in him. 11 Timothy 2: 15 Tell's you that study to show thy self approve unto God, a workman that needed not to be ashamed, rightly dividing the word of truth.

Also Job 13:15, through he slay me, yet will I trust in him: but I will maintain mine own way before God. As you read these words of the scripture, you will see that if you study the words of God, it will guide you into truth and righteousness. No matter how difficult life may seem to go through, If you learn to put your trust in Jesus Christ, he will never fail you, because he first love us. That's the reason why we as a sinful bean, can be able to love him back. We should learn to put our trust in him always. He helps us through all difficulties. When he went to the cross, he knew that he will be able to save his people. The responsibility was a great one for him to take, yet he over come, because he trust in his father. God responsibility is always a great one. The death of Jesus Christ could not be greater. When a person lay down his or her life for another! That could only be love. Love is the fulfillment of God Commandments. If we can show love one another and put our trust in Jesus Christ to take us through all things. It is possible, nothing is impossible in the sight of God. When God give one a responsibility to do his will, which mean you have to save people for the kingdom of God. Also help to save life through his healing power. That mean you do not6 used your self, Jesus used you, through his holy angels. Jesus is true, honest, peaceful, loving and kind hearted to others. Others must be able to trust in you. Through you is the chosen one. The world we are living in today is one that we as human bean have to be very careful in ever thing we do or say. There is only one person that can help any one to be able to do all these things. That person that God chosen have to be able to put his or her life in the hands of the only true and living God, of heaven and earth., the father son and Holy Ghost. The God of heaven and earth can used the Holy Ghost to learn you and guide you through all things that do or say. He can help you to be honest, loving, kind, caring, and all that is good. You have to let him in your heart, by loving him back, as he first love you. He never forests any one to love him. He show us that he love us all, by dying on the curial cross for us all. Colossians 3: 1- 4 tell you that, if ye then be risen with Christ, seek those things which are above, where Christ sitteth on the right hand of God. Set your affection on the on things above, not on things on the earth. For ye are dead, and your life is hid with Christ in God. When Christ, who is our life, shall appear, then shall ye also appear with him in Glory? St. John 14: 26, 27 SAID! But the comforter, which is the Holy Ghost, whom the father will send in my name, he shall teach you all things, and bring all things to your remembrance, whatsoever I have said unto you. Peace I leave with you, my peace I give unto you: not as the world giveth, give I unto you, let not your heart be troubled, neither let it be afraid. Also Acts. 1:8 tell you that! But ye shall receive power after that the Holy Ghost is come upon you: And ye shall be witnesses unto me both in Jerusalem, and in all Judea, and in Samaria, and unto the uttermost part of the earth. As you read these great words from the Bible, you can see that you can leave all things in the hands of God. He can lead, guide and detect all things in heaven, and on earth. Trust and obey Jesus! Daniel 4:1 Tell's you that, Neb-u-chad-nez-zar the king, unto all people, nations, and Languages, that dwell in all the earth; Peace be multiplied unto you. As you read this Scriptures, you can see that peace is what we all need in this world that we are living in to day. As we see the things that happening around us today. We all need to call unto the God of heaven and earth for peace in the entire world. The war in Iraq, hundred of people lost their lives, young men and women who just enter into the world of sin. They are trying to start a life of their own, before then even able to know the world they are living in, they die. The good Lord above knew all things. Put him first in your lives, by choosing him, and follow his words as you read them.

CHAPTER 6

PROBLEMS OF WHICH I COULD NOT UNDERSTAND

When a problem arrived in your life, and you know not what to do? It can be very difficult to deal with. But! When you have Jesus to call unto it can bring joy to your heart. There is a faith that is above every other faith, and that faith is Jesus, who walks on the Sea of Galilee. God open ways and means for me when there was now were to go. Because I have the unspeakable faith, I endure the difficult times. When Jesus walk on the Sea, he did not say a word, Peter only saw him walking on the Sea. That faith is from the God of heaven. Jesus said you should follow him; he has a faith that is above ever other faith. When I was turn out of my apartment, and have now where to go, Jesus send a messenger and open means for me so I could go some place that was safe for me and my daughter. Galatians 2: 16, 20, tell you that! Knowing that a man is not justified by the works of the Law, but by the faith of Jesus Christ, even we have believed in Jesus Christ, that we might be justified by the faith of Christ, and not by works of the Law: For by the works of the Law shall no flesh be justified. I am crucified with Christ: nevertheless I live: yet not I, but Christ liveth in me; and the life which I now live in the faith live of the son of God who loved me, and give himself for me. When we can have the faith like the son of God, which loved me, and gave his life for me, we will be able to over come all obstacles. Jesus believed in his father, that's the reason why he could be able to walk on the Sea with out sinking. Jesus faith in God is a mighty and a powerful one. Seek Jesus through his words and he will help you to have faith like him. I believe in Jesus, so when life seem hopeless, I have faith in him that he will make a way. Jesus never leaves his servant's to suffer. He will come to you in many different ways. I got a place to stay, and a few days later I call my Boss which I used to work for and told him my problem, and he told me where to go and I would get a job. I go to the nursing office, and I god a job the same day. That's the faith like Jesus walking on the Sea. Never give up, when life seems hope less. Jesus cares for us all; he will lead you into peace and happiness. Seek

Jesus faith and his love, before it's too late. Nehemiah 7; 2 Tell's you that I gave my brother Ha-na-ni and Han- a Ni-ah the ruler of the palace, charge over Jerusalem: for he was a faithful man, and feared God above many. Also 11 Thessalonians 1: 7,8 tell you that, and to who are troubled, rest with us, when the Lord Jesus shall be revealed from heaven with his mighty angels, in flaming fire taking vengeance on them that know not God, and that obey not the gospel of our Lord Jesus Christ. They will be punishing with fire. Jesus is our answer to our problems, whether they are big or small. When you over come by the blood of the lam! Jesus the savior, will always there to help you to overcome obstacle. You just have known that he is there, call on him in good times, trouble times, when your tears are flowing and when it's not flowing. He always here and answer prayer. I have gone through trying times, and when it's like I have come to the time when life seem hope less. I know there is a God that I can call on, I call on him and he brought me back to see that there is hope, and I should never give up. He takes me through, and has me going in full strength again. You should always put him first in your life. He loves you with on everlasting love. Your heart, and your mind, should always engage in God's words, so that if there is a time when you can only say Jesus. He will here and answers you, and he will also know you need him.

As you over come go to him and praise and give him thanks, for over coming power. He cares and he will be always there for you Jesus give us time to know him, to find him, to love him, and to overcome obstacles. We should accept the privilege he have granted unto us. Sometimes you will face with the drops of rain, sometime you will face with showers of rain, and sometimes you will face with storms, sometimes you will pass through the fire. Think of all these things. Who could help you to overcome those obstacles? Ask you're self, who could take me out of danger? The same beam that is unseen, that send the rain, the drop, the shower, he guide you through, because he used these trying times to let us know that there is a God that can guide you! And he can also destroy you and me. He is loving, kind, merciful and patient. Jonah 2: 1, 2, and 7-10 Tell's you that! Jonah prayed unto the lord his God out of the fish's belly, and said I cried by reason of mine affliction unto the Lord, and he heard me; out of the belly of hell cried I, and thou headrest my voice. When my soul fainted with in me I remember the Lord: and my prayer came in unto thee, into thine holy temple. They that observe lying vanities forsake their own mercy. But I will sacrifice unto thee with the voice of thanksgiving; I will pay that I have vowed, salvation is of the Lord. And the Lord spoke unto the fish and it vomited out Jonah upon the dry land. This is another experience I had! During the times of my problems I have change my eating and drinking many different meals; and drinking different tea and drinks. I went shopping one day at the supermarket, I saw a box of tea I pick up the box and start to read it to see what it was made from. The name was rose tea, on the box it said it was made from orange peel, and it had nosh's figurine in it. I start buying the tea and using it, each time I bought the box I got an animal in it. Until one day when I open one of the boxes, I got one figurine that was a man and a woman. I was so happy to see that two people were saved. I got 30 animals and only two people. I ask the question! How many people will be able to be saved in God kingdom? Will it be like Noah's days? I know that was a sign from God to me and others. The same way all the animal was going into the bout is the same way I received them. Jesus needs us to answer his calling before it is too late. Noah was warning the people about the rain, and telling then what would have happen. No one take heed of what was happening, until the flood came and wash them all away. Jesus sends his messenger to tell you all to be ready before his second coming. It will be more dangerous, he is coming with brim stone and fire, be ye ready! Jesus is coming soon. Let these signs lead you into righteousness. Jesus loves us with on everlasting love. Follow his words and let him into your hearts. Matthew 12: 39,-41 tell you that! But he answered and said unto them. An evil and adulterous generation seeketh after a sign and there shall no sign be given to it, but the sign of the prophet Jonas. For as Jonas was three days and three nights in the whale's belly; so shall the son of man be three days and three nights in the hearts of the earth. The men of Nineveh shall rise in Judgment with this generation, and shall condemn it: because they repented at the preaching of Jonas: And behold, a grater than Jonas is here. As you read these scriptures you will see that the only signs you will fallow or learn from are signs of the prophets. So be ye ready! Jesus is near. Follow the teaching of God's servants, before it's too late. After reading these verses of scriptures you can understand what I am saying about calling on the Lord, even in the rain or in fire, he will here and answer prayer. Sometimes you go to the sea side to have a swim or a walk, and when you look across and you can see the wave's rolling over very heavy. It's scared you some times. You would like to go in, but it's seemed too dangerous for you. And there came another time when you would look at the sea and it become very calm and you would go right in and have lots of fun in the water. Jesus is the only one who can be able to let all those things happen, he is the great and mighty God of heaven and earth. We know that he is there because we can see the things that he can do. Some times you looked at the sea and you feel as you can walk on it. Because it seem as steady as if you would be able to walk on the Sea of Galilee, and try to walk and water like Jesus did. You can plant a seed in the earth and watch it grew from a seed to a tree and even bring fruits, as a result you can eat or make drinks from it. We should know that there is a beam higher than us, that we can not see. But because of the great and mighty things that we can see around us happening we should know that he is alive and watching over us. He loves us, that's why we need to serve Jesus. In august of 1992 we had on hurricane which hit Miami, and another state. There were a lot of people loose their homes, cars, and all that they had work for over the years. That's a great deal of thing for any one to overcome. I feel it very bad for them, for the reason that I have experience lost as well. Therefore I know how difficult it is. It helps me to get closer with Jesus Christ. I do anticipate every one will take these signs as a warning, and make an effort to acquire to discern Jesus, as a result that when these things happen, we will be able to over come through his words, with problems like these. Jesus will soon come! And we all need him. Jesus our savior strength of character, in a little while is coming; I said to my self, I know he will not let me be in danger of hell fire; he will help me to be faithful in him continually. He promises to acquire me out of every danger if I trust and fair his mighty name! When I come home from church the land lady ask me if I got a place. I said no! I went back to church, and spend the after noon at the meeting. So I keep praying in my heart that the good Lord will soon work out a way for me to get a place to live. I come to realize that I am a child of God, and these are some of the things that will test my faith with God. When I was about 18 years of age, I have my first vision, about the Ten Commandments. I keep it in my memory, but I did not exercise it as strong as I ought to. When I was 30 years of age I had my second vision of which I also kept in my brain. It was about preaching in a Church, and what I should drink for my health. I did make an effort to make use of the health part of the vision. Not knowing it was so important for me to perform as I was told. Therefore I keep going on with my life with out doing them. Matthew 7: 26 Tell's you that any one here my voice and do it not, shall be like the man that build his house upon a sand. Jesus voice can comes in many different ways. Therefore we should endeavor to distinguish him in the true way. He is sure, true and loving and you can trust him, he will never allow you to go down. And Jesus said! You should not with drown your self from the world in order to escape from persecution. Come to Jesus as you are for the reason that you found him and love him. Persecution will always come any were you are. Each and every one need to go in the direction of trusting in Jesus Christ and prays always and request of Jesus to guide you through every things you do are say. When you have Jesus with you; you will for eternity love every body, even when they are against you. And you will always desire to help them too. In the direction of being a child of God, you ought to go throughout life with trial and tribulations. I know people who have done me wrong and yet I love them all the same! With Jesus love you should not hate any one. That's one of the reason I know I am a follower of Jesus Christ. He will soon to approach us in the clouds; we ought to endeavor to discover his goodness and grace. I find him at the age of 41 years of age, and I promise to present to him the rest of my life on earth to serve him, and help others to know him. Now I have come to the time when I have to face the world and tell them about God wonderful work according to the Bible, I have to be ordained to speak to others in the sanctuary. I have to go into special prayer and care for my body! This is the vision I had about the garlic and Guinean weed come in. Jesus is the only answer for my work. Jesus is a Miracle working savior. He can perform great things. When you think of a mother who has conceived and bring forth a child in her womb for nine month is that a wonderful thing? I could remember when I start having my children, I always planning for them and saying how many children I would like to have, not knowing that God have plans for me. I even stop my self with a Doctor from having children. And God open my child bearing womb by giving me two additional kids, in the direction of proving to me how great he is. I did not know from my mother, that God has given me to my mother as a special gift. Therefore God planed for me! Jesus can direct the way for each and every one of us, if we only give permission to him to have a place in our hearts. No matter how heard it may seem. I love him yet more when I come to know him, and know that he was the one who always maintain me through all the terrible times. I actually desire to enlighten others with the love of Jesus. I am praying that he will open every door for me, to tell others about Jesus through this book, and redeem you of al things. Jesus is the savior who you can depend on. He cares for us all. He first cares for us, which are why he went to the cross for us. The love that he had for us is a very great one. The Lord will never leave any of his creatures; he watches all of us with loving care. You are his creature and he cares for you. Jesus said seek him and you shall find him, knock and it shall be open unto you. Deuteronomy 4: 29 tell you that, but if from thence thou shalt seek the Lord thy God, thou shalt find him with all thy heart and with all thy soul. As you read these words, you can see that if you would only seek him ye will here you, and save you from all your sins. He cares for us all, this is how good he is to me. Gen.12: 1-3 Tell's me that when Jesus wants his Prophets to do his work, he will move you to a land where he will make your name great. Sometimes when you are with your own people It's seems so difficult to enlighten them with the love of Jesus. Therefore that's why Jesus will put you what ever place he can use you to accomplish his work. Writing this book is one of my ways of telling others how wonderful Jesus can be to each and ever one of his people. When a person get a brain from God! That's a special blessing from God! You should use it with special care. Using your brain to do the thing which is not right is a very incorrect thing to do. We should always use it in the will of our Lord and savior Jesus Christ. And ask him to help you to do ever thing that you would like to do. Your brain is a very important part of your body! God should always be the director of it. The responsibility of God work is a great one! God work is saving souls! Jesus dies on the cross to acquire away our sins. How can we as human beans not show love and honesty to one another? When a person of God's aptitude working to save souls and lives, they should be honest, that others can trust them, Jesus need honest, inflexible working people to perform his work. Jesus work is a fundamental one; we should follow his words carefully. He suffers and dies so we can endeavor to be sanctified as he is. Jesus cares for us, and he desires us to care for others as well. My baby daughter came in this world in a very critical time in my life. The way in witch she came was a very crucial way! I have to make that decision to have her in a manner that hurt; I know that it would bring pain to my heart. However I had to have her for the reason that the child was needed in my work to help me conquer the tribal tribulation I was face with. Satan was in the midst, and God require a special angel in my life to be of assistance to help me over come. I have overcome, and the child has grown to be a woman. I give God thanks, to show me such great and mighty work. I want to continue to praise the soon coming king, until he comes. Although I can not stand to see a child like that been hurt. All my children have been hurt because of the problems. The pains of children being hurt give me pain workman that needed not to be ashamed if you learn to put your trust in Jesus Christ, he will never fail you, because he first love us. That's the reason why he walks a part and asks us to follow him. Jesus dies to take away all our sins. So we can be clean, and be able to enter into his father's kingdom. Jesus first love's us so we will as a sin- full human bean can be able to love him also. He gave us his words, so we will be able to read them and understand them, and follow his foot step. Why not serve him now? Jesus knows us by name and nature; he knows ever hair that grew on our heads. Don't you think he cares for us all? He is our savior! He never failed, Jesus never leaves you. You just of to put him in your hearts and he will help you to need him. His words can love us with on everlasting love. That's the reason why he dies for us, so he can save us from our sins. When you become a savior for others, you will seek ever journey to save one's life. Jesus father see the world we are living in, and that was the only solution he could find to save his people. God love us with on everlasting love. That's why he gave his life for us. Jeremiah 31:3 Tell's you that the Lord hath appeared of old unto me, saying, yea, I have loved thee with an everlasting love; therefore with an loving kindness have I drawn thee. Also John 15: 13, Tell's you that, greater love hath no man than this, that a man lay down his life for his friends. We should learn to put our trust in him always. He helps us through all difficulties. When he went to the cross, he knew that he will be able to save his people. The responsibility was a great one for him to take, yet he over come, because he trust in his father. God responsibility is always a great one. The death of Jesus Christ could not be greater, when a person lay down his or her life for his friend that is great. As you read these verses of scripture, you can see that Jesus love us. He cares! And he wants us to be saved in his kingdom. He will give you the time to know him, to follow him, to put your trust in him, and believed in him. Jesus loved you with on everlasting love, he never change. Trust in him and fare him. He knows no sin! He did no wrong. Jesus had done what his father wants him to do. The father knew that there would be now other way to save his people, whom he love, he care's for us all and want us to be save in his father's kingdom. When he went to the cross, he knew that his father would rise him up again to be great leader for his people. So he laid his life into his hands. He believes in his father. And trust in him. He is able to give us overcoming powder, to over come all obstacles. He dies for us so we need to fear him and trust in him with all our hearts. Job 13: 15 tell us that, though he slays me yet will I trust him; but I will maintain mine own ways before him. Job 39: 11 wilt thou trust him because his strength is great? Or wilt thou leave thy labor to him. There is time's we may stray from only son to save us. Why not serve him? He first loves you. You can return to him your love, by serving him. He cares! Serve him. Serving him! Is praising him in songs and praying. Give your heart to him so he can use you in a special way. Jesus is love in actions! Jesus is real! When one life seems like its falling, never give us, because of difficult times. I was staying by one of my church sister home; she gave me one of sister E.G. white book, I read it and it was very interesting to learn more about Jesus words, and to know there is hope. There was a telephone number in the book, I call that number, and ask for another chapter. They send me the voice of props icy lesion. I take that lesion, and was certified for 26 lessons. A few weeks later I received other lesions on Daniel. The reading of Daniel inspired me in such a way so I gather strength to hold on even stronger in the name of Jesus. Jesus is reel! Never let any problem get you down. Keep your heart fix on Jesus, through all ruff times, and good times. He cares! I can tell you that there is sometimes it will seem hopeless, you will even ask you're self why life seems hopeless? There is a name that is above every other name. Seek for that name and put him in your heart and mind. The world we are living in today, seem hopeless. But Jesus will step in and show us that there is a name above ever other name. The hurricane's that come upon us and take all we have and even take lives, that's the gratis signs that show to us that there is a name we need to call upon. He wants us to know that he is among us and we need to find him and serve him. He is very near! His words tell us that he very near. Act's 24: 25 tell you that, and as he reasoned of righteousness, temperance, and judgment to come, Felix trembled. And answered go thy way for this time; when I have convenient season, I will call for thee. Jesus say's in Matthew 25: 34 then shall the king say unto them on his right hand, come, ye blessed of my father inherit the kingdom prepared for you from the foundation of the world. Also in Daniel 4: 3 tell you that, how great are his signs! And how mighty are his wonders! His kingdom is an everlasting kingdom, and his dominion is from generation to generation, According to the reading of these great scriptures, you can see that Jesus is coming to redeem his people that are ready, to be with him in his Kingdom, on his right hand. We should take the signs that we are seeing today, and try to be ready for Jesus when he comes. Jesus is at the door let him in. That could only be love. Love is the fulfillment of God Commandments. If we can show love to others and put our trust in Jesus Christ to take us through all things. It is possible, nothing is impossible in the sight of God. When God give one a responsibility to do his will, which mean you have to save people for the kingdom of God. Also help to save life through his healing power. That mean you do not6 used your self, Jesus used you, through his holy angels. Jesus is true, honest, peaceful, loving and kind hearted to others. Others must be able to trust in you. Through you is the chosen one. The world we are living in today is one that we as human bean have to be very careful in ever thing we do or say. There is only one person that can help any one to be able to do all these things. That person that God chosen have to be able to put his or her life in the hands of the only true and living God of heaven and earth, the father son and Holy Ghost. The God of heaven and earth can used the Holy Ghost to learn you and guide you through all things that do or say. He can help you to be honest, loving, kind, caring, and all that is good. You have to let him in your heart, by loving him back, as he first love you. He never stops any one from loving him. He show us that he love us all, by dying on the curial cross for us each and every one. Colossians 3: 1-4 tell you that, if ye then be raised with Christ, seek those things which are above, where Christ sited on the right hand of God. Set your affection on the things above, not on things on the earth. For ye are dead, and your life is hid with Christ in God. When Christ, who is our life, shall appear then shall ye appear with him in Glory? St. John 14: 26 SAID! But the comforter, which is the Holy Ghost, whom the father will send in my name, he shall teach you all things, and bring all things to your remembrance, what so ever I have said unto you. Peace I leave with you, my peace I give unto you: not as the world giveth, give I unto you, let not your heart be troubled, neither let it be afraid. Also Acts. 1:8 tell you that, but ye shall received power after that the Holy Ghost is come upon you: Ye shall be witnesses unto me both in Jerusalem, and in all Judea, and in Sa-mar-i-a, and unto the uttermost part of the earth. As you read these great words from the Bible, you can see that you can leave all things in the hands of God. He can lead, guide and detect all things on earth and in heaven. Trust and obey Jesus! Daniel 4:1 Tell's you that, Neb-u-ch-ad-nez-zar the king, unto all people, nations, and Languages, that dwell in all the earth; Peace be multiplied unto you. As you read this Scriptures, you can see that peace is what we all need in this world that we are living in today. As we see the things that happening around us today, we all need to call unto the God of heaven and earth for peace in the entire world. The hostilities in Iraq, hundred of people lost their lives, young men and women who just enter into the world of sin, they are trying to start a life of their own, before they even able to know the world they are living in, they die. The superior Lord above knew every thing! Therefore we can only have faith in him, knowing with the intention of we be able to serve him, he will save us.

Problem that needs to be solves, through the understanding of God and none other. When God let you have a child, there should be tender care in bringing up that child. God can let you be a child for his services. There should be tender care given to that person, try to know him or her as they accept Jesus Christ as their personal savior from sin. To do God will is very important. When that person become a child of again, it become a child again, it become a very critical problem for that person. Jesus alone and his Angels can communicate with that person. With out Jesus give someone the understanding to communicate with that person, it's much heard for any one to help him or her. We should first have love for every one, so that Jesus can help others to help when there is a problem. Jesus Christ is love. Try to seek him first into your lives, so you can know him, and understand others when Jesus is using them. When Jesus let you become a child again, he needs you for a special reason. He has to train you as if you were training a baby to be on adult. So he or she can go into the world to earn a living. When Jesus is training an adult, that become a child again, he need that person to become on adult to go out into the world of sin to bring people into his kingdom. He needs you to prepare the way for his second coming. He needs you to have a clear mind. So you can deliver his massage to his people. He will be speaking to that person from time to time. Jesus messenger are specially trained. When the training is enforced to that person if they do not have understanding, and able to follow rules, you can loose your mind. Jesus and his angels are that person strength at that moment. So we can see others need, and help them through Jesus love. Jesus said in Exodus 20: 6, and show mercy unto thousand of them that love me and keep my commandments. According to this scripture, Jesus wants us to sow mercy to thousand that love him and keep his commandments. So when you have Jesus you will be able to help others. Jesus is love! Seek him first in your lives. When you find Jesus you find gold and purity. Gold gives you love purity, and piece.

With God help all things are possible, I was coming from work one night, and it was pouring rain, the Holy Spirit came upon me in such a way that I had to pull off the road and answer to the voice of Jesus; he gave me strength to go on each day and time. I came to realize that he needs me to follow his words. I answer by started to read his words. I read them every day, and I come to him through baptizing. The experience I had was very fighting. Only the good Lord could help me to over come the way I was feeling. I always cry when I feel that way. But as I come to know that it was Jesus calling, I learn to trust in him. If we just learn to trust Jesus and love him, he will help us in all things that we face. "Jesus is the way! He is the only way." I would like every one to try and know Jesus. It seems much heard some times, because there is lot of test and trial. When those times come around, you have to do is turn to Jesus in prayer. When you can pray, it can really bring joy to your heart. You can speak to Jesus just as you would speak to a friend. Tell Jesus how you feel; tell him what you need, ask him to help you to know him, and love him. He will here you and answer prayer! Jesus wants you to come to him just as you are, with all your problems. He will help you! Put Jesus in your heart and feel his love for you. When you love him? And learn to trust him, that's the reason he will always here your prayer. He cares, let him in and ask him to help you. He had done that for me, and I know he will do the same for you. Jesus knows every one of us, when we have bad times and good times. Some times these things happen. "Jesus can help us to turn to him." We should not wait until bad times come around." We should try to find him now, before it's too late. If the bad times come before we find him, he will understand. Some of us always never stop to think about Jesus when we have good times. So when the bad times come that's the time we seems to look for Jesus. He will always help you, "go to him in bad times or good times. He will always answer your prayer." He cares for us all! And he wants us to be saved in his kingdom.

He will not push you to come to him! He let you make your own mind up, which way you want to go. There is two ways! The choice is yours. All he asks you to do is to follow his words carefully. He cares so much that he dies on the cross to save us from our sins. He do ever thing that is possible to show us the right way. Jesus way, come to him, he is pleading for you and for me. As you read this book I do hope it will inspire your hearts, and help you to see Jesus clearer. I would like others to come to Jesus before it is too late, that's why I wrote this book. I have suffered to know this calling. He has called me in many different ways, before I say yes. After I start to suffer that's the time I remember his calling and realize that it was Jesus calling me, to do his will and obey his words. I have to give him praise ever day to come to know him and acknowledge his calling. So I would like every one who reads this book to hasting to his call now, before it's too late. Please give him some attention, to his calling and come to him before it's too late. If Jesus want you to work for him, and you do not accept his calling, he can let it be through suffering. I would not like any one to suffer the way I have to know his calling was important. Some times the easy way to know him is to listen to others. When they tell you about the love of God, try to understand, and read the word of God for your self. Obedience is the best way to know Jesus! If we can be obedience we will yeal to others. And try to understand God's words. If you understand what Jesus want you to do, you will always want to do his will. Sometimes it is not easy for you to understand others, you need to try read for your self, and have faith and his love, before it's too late. Nehemiah 7; 2 Tell's you that I gave my brother Ha-na-ni and Han- a Ni-ah the ruler of the palace, charge over Jerusalem: for he was a faithful man, and feared God above many. Also 11 Thessalonians 1: 7,8 tell you that, and to who are troubled, rest with us, when the Lord Jesus shall be revealed from heaven with his mighty angels, in flaming fire taking vengeance on them that know not God, and that obey not the gospel of our Lord Jesus Christ. They will be punishing with fire. Jesus is our answer to our problems, whether they are big or small. When you over come by the blood of the lam! Jesus the savior, will constantly there to help you to overcome obstacle. You just have to known that he is there, call on him in good times, trouble times, when your tears are flowing and when it's not flowing. He always here and answer prayer. I have gone through trying times, and when it's like I have come to the time when life seem hopeless. I know there is a God that I can call on, I call on him and he brought me back to see that there is hope, and I must never give up. He takes me through, and has me going in full strength again. You should at all times put him first in your life. He loves you with on everlasting love. Your heart, and your mind, should constantly engage in God's words, as a result that if there is a time when you can only say Jesus. He will here and answers you, and he will also know you need him.

As you over come go to him and praise his matchless name and give him thanks, for over coming power. He cares and he will be for eternity there for you, Jesus give us time to know him, to find him, to love him, and to overcome obstacles. We should accept the privilege he have granted unto us. Sometimes you will face with the drops of rain, sometime you will face with showers of rain, and sometimes you will face with storms, sometimes you will pass through the fire. Think of all these things. Who could help you to overcome those obstacles? Ask yourself, who could take me out of danger? The same Jesus that is unseen, that send the rain, the drop, the showers, he guide you through, for the reason that he used these trying times to let us know that there is a God that can guide you! And he can also destroy you and me. He is loving, kind, merciful and patient. Jonah 2: 1, 2, and 7-10 Tell's you that! Jonah prayed unto the Lord his God out of the fish belly, and said I cried by reason of mine affliction unto the Lord, and he heard me; out of the belly of hell cried I, and thou headrest my voice. When my soul fainted with in me I remember the Lord: and my prayer came in unto thee, into thine holy temple. They that observe lying vanities forsake their own mercy. But I will sacrifice unto thee with the voice of thanksgiving; I will pay that I have vowed, salvation is of the Lord. And the Lord spoke unto the fish and it vomited out Jonah upon the dry land. This is another experience I had! During the times of my problems I have change my eating and drinking many different meals; and drinking different tea and drinks. I went shopping one day at the supermarket, I saw a box of tea I pick up the box and start to read it to see what it was made from. The name was rose tea, on the box it said it was made from orange peal, and it had nosh's figurine in it. I start buying the tea and using it, each time I bought the box I got an animal in it. Until one day when I open one of the boxes, I got one figurine that was a man and a woman. I was so happy to see that two people were saved. I got 30 animals and only two people. I ask the question about what you do not understand. You can pray and ask the good Lord to help you to understand his words. Jesus shows me himself in vision. So if you really want's to know Jesus just ask him to help you! How many people will be able to be saved in God kingdom? Will it be like Noah's days? I know that was a sign from God to me and others. The same way all the animal was going into the bout is the same way I received them. Jesus needs us to answer his calling before it is too late. Noah was warning the people about the rain, and telling then what would have happen. No one take heed of what was happening, until the flood came and wash them all away. Jesus sends his messenger to tell you each and every one to be ready before his second coming.

It will be more dangerous, he is coming with brim stone and fire, be ye ready! Jesus is coming soon. Let these signs lead you into righteousness'. Jesus loves us with on everlasting love. Follow his words and let him into your hearts. Matthew 12: 39,-41 tell you that, but he answered and said unto them, an evil and adulterous generation seeketh after a sign and there shall no sign be given to it, but the sign of the prophet Jonas. For as Jonas was three days and three nights in the whale's belly; so shall the son of man be three days and three nights in the hearts of the earth. The men of Nineveh shall rise in Judgment with this generation, and shall condemn it: because they repented at the preaching of Jonas: And behold, a grater than Jonas is here. As you read these scriptures you will see that the only signs you will fallow or learn from are signs of the prophets. Therefore be ye ready! Jesus is near. Follow the teaching of God's servants, before it's too late. After reading these verses of scriptures you can understand what I am saying about calling on the Lord, even in the rain or in fire, he will here and answer prayer. Sometimes you go to the sea side to have a swim or a walk, and when you look across and you can see the wave's rolling over very heavy. It's scared you some times. You would like to go in, but it's seemed too dangerous for you. And there came another time when you would look at the sea and it become very calm and you would go right in and have lots of fun in the water. Jesus is the solitary one who is capable of being able to let all those things happen, he is the great and mighty God of heaven and earth. We know that he is there for the reason that we can observe the things that he can do. Some times you looked at the sea and you feel as you can walk on it, for the reason that it seem as steady as if you would be able to walk on the Sea of Galilee, you can plant a seed in the earth and watch it grew from a seed to a tree and even bring fruits. As a result you can eat or make drinks from it. We should know that there is supernatural beam higher than us, that we can not see. However for the reason that of the great and mighty things that we can see around us happening we should know that he is alive and watching over us. He love us that why he walk all the way by dying for us, and ask us to follow him. Jesus dies to take away all our sins. Therefore we can be clean, and be able to enter into his father's kingdom. Jesus first love's us as a result we will be able to love him as well. He gave us his words, as a result we will be able to read them and understand them, and follow his foot step. Why not serve him now? Jesus knows us by name and nature; he knows ever hair that grew on our heads. Don't you think he cares for us all? He is our savior!

Jeremiah 31:3 Tell's you that the Lord hath appeared of old unto me, saying, yea, I have loved thee with an everlasting love; therefore with a loving kindness have I drawn thee. Also John 15: 13, Tell's you that, greater love hath no man than this, that a man lay down his life for his friends. As you read these verses of scripture, you can see that Jesus love us. He cares! And he wants us to be saved in his kingdom. He will give you the time to know him, to follow him, to put your trust in him, and believed in him. Jesus loved you with on everlasting love, he never change. Trust in him and fare him! He knows no sin! He did no wrong. Jesus did what his father wants him to accomplish. The father knew that there would be now other way to save his people, whom he love, he care's for us all and want us to be save in his father's kingdom. When he went to the cross, he knew that his father would rise him up again to be great leader for his people. Therefore he laid his life into his hands. He believes in his father. And trust in him. He is able to give us overcoming powder, on the way to over come each and every obstacle. He dies for us therefore we need to fear him and trust in him with all our hearts. Job 13: 15 tell us that, though he slays me yet will I trust him; but I will maintain mine own ways before him. Job 39: 11 wilt thou trust him because his strength is great? Or wilt thou leave thy labor to him. There is time's we may stray from his house of worship, nevertheless Jesus never leaves you. You just of to put him in your heart and he will help you to need him. His words can redeem you of all things. Jesus is the savior who you can depend on. He cares for us all. He first cares for us, which are why he went to the cross for us. The love that he had for us is a very great one. The Lord will never leave any of his creatures; he watches each and every one of us with loving care. You are his creature and he cares for you. Jesus said seek him and you shall find him, knock and it shall be open unto you. Deuteronomy 4: 29 tell you that, but if from thence thou shalt seek the Lord thy God, thou shalt find him with all thy heart and with all thy soul. As you read these words, you can see that if you would only seek him ye will here you, and save you from all your sins. He cares for us all, he love us with on everlasting love. That's the reason why he dies for us; as a result he can save us from our sins. When you become a savior for others, you will seek increasingly journey to save one's life. Jesus father see the world we are living in, and that was the only solution he could find to save his people. God love us with on everlasting love. That's why ye gave his only son to save us. Why not serve him? He first loves you. You can return to him your love, by serving him. He cares! Serve him. Serving him!

Is praising him in songs and praying. Give your heart to him accordingly he can use you in a special way to save others. Jesus is love in actions! Jesus is real! When one life seems like its falling, never give up, for the reason of difficult times. I was staying by one of my church sister home; she gave me one of sister E.G. white book, I read it and it was very interesting to learn more about Jesus words, and to know there is hope. There was a telephone number in the book, I call that number, and ask for another chapter of the book. They send me the corresponding course from the Bible school, it is written lesion! I take that lesion, and was certified for 26 lessons. A few weeks later I received other lesions on Daniel. The reading of Daniel inspired me in such a way as a result I gather strength to hold on stronger in the name of Jesus. Jesus is reel! Never let any problem get you down. Keep your heart fix on Jesus, through all ruff times, and good times. He cares! I can tell you that there is sometimes it will seem hopeless, you will sometimes ask your self why life seems hopeless? There is a name that is above every other name. Seek for that name and put him in your heart and mind. The world we are living in today, seem hopeless. But Jesus will step in and show us that there is a name above ever other name. The hurricane's that come upon us and take all we have and even take lives, that's the greatest signs that show to us that there is a name we need to call upon. He wants us to know that he is among us and we need to find him and serve him. He is very near! His words tell us that he very near. Act's 24: 25 tell you that, and as he reasoned of righteousness, temperance, and judgment to come, Felix trembled. And answered go thy way for this time; when I have convenient season, I will call for thee. Jesus say's in Matthew 25: 34 then shall the king say unto them on his right hand, come, ye blessed of my father inherit the kingdom prepared for you from the foundation of the world. Also in Daniel 4: 3 tell you that, how great are his signs! And how mighty are his wonders! His kingdom is an everlasting kingdom, and his dominion is from generation to generation, According to the reading of these great scriptures, you can see that Jesus is coming to redeem his people that are ready, to be with him in his Kingdom, on his right hand. We should take the signs that we are seeing today, and try to be ready for Jesus when he comes. Jesus is at the door let him in.

Problem that needs to be solves, through the understanding of God and none other. When God let you have a child, there should be tender care in bringing up that child. God can let you be a child for his services. There should be tender care given to that person, try to know him or her as they accept Jesus Christ as their personal savior from sin. To do God will is very important. When that person becomes a child again, it becomes a very critical problem for that person. Jesus alone and his Angels can communicate with that person. With out Jesus give someone the understanding to communicate with that person, it's a great deal for any one to help him or her. We should first have love for every one; consequently that Jesus can help others to help when there is a problem. Jesus Christ is love. Try to seek him first into your lives, as a result you can know him, and understand others when Jesus is using them. When Jesus let you become a child again, he needs you for a special reason. He has to train you as if you were training a baby to be on adult. Therefore he or she can go into the world to perform his work and earn a living. When Jesus is training an adult, that become a child again, he need that person to become on adult to go out into the world of sin to bring people into his kingdom. He needs you to prepare the way for his second coming. He needs you to have a clear mind. As a result you can deliver his massage to his people. He will be speaking to that person from time to time. Jesus messenger are specially trained. When the training is enforced to that person if they do not have understanding, and able to follow rules, you can loose your mind. Jesus and his angels are that person strength at that moment. Therefore we can see others need, and help them through Jesus love. Jesus said in Exodus 20: 6, and showing mercy unto thousand of them that love me and keep my commandments. According to this scripture, Jesus wants us to sow mercy to thousand that love him and keep his commandments. Therefore as soon as you have Jesus in your heart, you will be able to help others. Jesus is love! Seek him first in your lives. When you find Jesus you find joyfulness' and purity. Joyfulness gives you love purity, and piece.

CHAPTER 7
EXPERIENCE I HAD WITH GOD'S HELP!

With God help all things are possible, I was coming from work one night, and it was pouring rain, the Holy Spirit came upon me in such a way that I had to pull off the road and answer to the voice of Jesus; he gave me strength in the direction to go on each day and find him. I came to realize that he needs me to follow his words. I answer by started to read his words. I read them every day, and I draw closer to him through baptizing. The experience I had was very fighting. Only the good Lord could help me to over come the way I was feeling. I constantly cry when I feel that way! But as I come to know that it was Jesus calling, I learn to trust in him. If we just learn to trust Jesus and love him, he will help us in all things that we face. "Jesus is the way! He is the only way." I would like every one to make an effort and know Jesus. It seems a great deal sometimes, for the reason that there is lot of ordeal and trial. When those times come in the region of testing, you have to turn to Jesus in prayer. As soon as you can pray, it can actually bring joyfulness to your heart. You can speak to Jesus just as you would speak to a friend. Tell Jesus how you feel; tell him what you need, ask him to help you to know him, and love him. He will here you and answer prayer! Jesus desires you to come to him just as you are, with each and every one of your problems. Jesus will help you! Put Jesus in your heart and feel his love for you. When you love him, and learn to trust him that's how he wills for eternity here your prayer. Jesus cares, let him in and ask him to be of assistance to your needs. He had done that for me, and I know he will do the same for you. Jesus knows every one of us, when we have terrible times and excellent times. Sometimes these things happen. "Jesus can help us to turn to him." We should not wait until bad times come in the order to call unto him." We should endeavor to discover him now, before it's too late. If the terrible times come before we discover him, he will understand. Some of us constantly never think about Jesus when we have excellent times. Therefore when the terrible times come, that's the time we seem turn toward looking for Jesus. He will for eternity facilitate your needs, "Seek to find him in dreadful times or excellent times. He will constantly answer your prayer." Jesus cares for us all! And he desires us to be saved in his kingdom. "Jesus Christ! He is Love, caring, kind, patient, and peaceful". "Jesus is a sure one, he never failed". Just ask him to come into your heart, and assist you to know him. He will not force you to come to him! He allows you to formulate your personal intellect to come to know him, and to know which way you desire to follow Jesus or Satan. "There is two ways! The choice is yours." All Jesus requests you to accomplish, is to follow his words carefully. He cares so much that he dies on the cross to save us from our sins. Jesus execute ever thing that is possible to show us the right way. Jesus is the way, come to him, he is pleading for you and for me. As you read this book I do anticipate it will inspire your hearts, and help you to see Jesus clearer. I would like others in the direction of trying to find Jesus come to know Jesus before it's too late, that's why I wrote this book. I have suffered to know this calling. Jesus has called me in many different ways, before I say yes. After I start to suffer that's the time I remember his calling and realize that it was Jesus calling me, to perform his will and obey his words. I have to give him praise ever day, for the reason that he has assisted me to come to know him and acknowledge his calling. Therefore I would like every one who reads this book to hasting to his call now, before it's too late. Please give him some attention, toward his calling as well as come to him before it's too late. If Jesus want you to work for him, and you do not accept his calling, he can let it be through suffering. I would not like any one to suffer the technique I have to know his calling was important. Sometimes the simple approach to know Jesus is to listen to others, when they tell you about the love of God, tries to understand, and read the word of God for your self. Obedience is another best approach to know Jesus! If we can be obedience and humble in our hearts, we will listen to others who Tell's us about Jesus words, and try to understand God's words. If you understand what Jesus desire you to accomplish, you will for all time desire to perform his will. Sometimes it's not easy for you to understand others, you need to try read for your self, and ask question about what you do not understand. You can pray and ask the good Lord to be of assistance to you, in the direction of understand his words. Jesus shows me himself in vision. Therefore if you really desire to know Jesus just ask him to assist you. He loves you and care for you.

CHAPTER 8

ACCEPTING GOD'S CALLING

When I finally come to know Jesus and accept his calling through baptizing. I decided to get baptize, it was a great experience for me. I always constantly was told by my mother and others to get baptized; I always say I was not equipped to be baptized. Yet I told them I wanted was to acquire baptism on my own. I also said! At what time I decided to be baptized, I will not turn back. After I did it, it was surprised when I go to visit church on that Sabbath morning. It was the 15th of December 1991; I really take it up actually obtain it on my own. Only the good Lord could let me do so. As soon as I see God work to do execute, I could not say no to God's calling. I got baptize on the same day, after the mid day service. Jesus was the only solitary could let me take that important step with out thinking about it. It was me and Jesus who went down into the baptism pool with my arms stretch out just as if I was on the cross. It makes me happy to know Jesus, and to discern he can work miracles. I would like every one to try make an effort for Jesus and he will allow you to have the same experience. I constantly say marriage and baptism are very important vows. I know if Jesus did not desire to give us a free choice, he could have let me take up baptism a long time ago. He is a just patient God, a loving and kind God. When you request Jesus to give permission to do the right thing, he is always for eternity there for you. He really shows me the approach to follow his words. It was not easy; I know am acquainted with him through trial and tribulation. I think that's one of his ways to prove to his people that he is the true and living God. It's a much work to accomplish; I would advice that the first step to take is in the direction of seeking to find Jesus and "love Jesus Christ with all your heart." Sometimes it will take time to give him all your heart, just ask him to help you, to follow his words. Let Jesus into your heart and tell him you love him, and that you desire to serve him. Tell him all about each and every one about your problems, and ask him to help you to overcome. Jesus loves each and every one of us and he desires to help us all. If you just permit him in! Sometimes you will even give Jesus your heart through baptism and start going to church, and you will see things that are not right. The first thing that will come to your intellect is to leave and go back into the world of sin. But nevertheless if you put Jesus love first into your heart and have faith through him, he will be there in attendance more to help you go on and follow him. Just immediately follow Jesus through his love. As you say yes to him in baptism! Jesus is the only one who helps me to keep going on through terrible times. When you go to him and give your heart, that's the time Satan followers will try attempt to get a hold of you, you should try to have Jesus in your heart, so that he will never over power you. Jesus is the answer! Just love you, trust him and pray constantly "He will deliver you just as he did for me. Keep him in your heart with a song". Sometimes I know it's not easy to have Jesus in your heart, but however I found Jesus to be the only cure for problems. The only way to get hurting and suffering out of you is through the love of God. I have spoke to a church brother, who told me he has become a Seventh day Adventist recently, and in a short time after he had got Baptize, he stop going to Church, because he did not believe with some things, and some of the people in the church is worst of than the people in the world of sin. I have to encourage him to keep going and try to help in any way to bring people to God, I told him I have the same experience, and try to leave, but Jesus would not let me. Jesus got a hold and pulls me back in. I was so hurt because of what I see was happening in the church I just wanted to leave. But God show me that he sent me to help the people of God to overcome. I could only keep praying to God for strength to be there. Isaiah 19: 20 Said! And it shall be for a sign and for a witness unto the Lord of hosts in the land of Egypt: for they shall cry unto the Lord because of the oppressors, and he shall send them a saviour, and a great one, and he shall deliver them. I have God in a mighty way. I could not contain myself, only God could deliver me from stop crying. And after reading this text I come to realize that God was using me in a mighty way to deliver his people. Also Matthew 10: 40 Said! He that receiveth you receiveth me, and he that receiveth me receiveth him that sent me. Only have faith in Jesus and believe in him. (I had another experience of Pain with in me; I have been away from my son for over 11.5 years, before I see him. When I spoke to him these was his words! Mammy I am hurting so much, I do not even have too many friends, because I am longing to see you. He became a child of God and that's what keeps me going on in life. God's love, he said is mammy's love, because he visited three churches of which I cry out to is close to my heart as mammy's heart. Therefore because he feels the love of God in his heart, that's the strength that keeps him until, I went and see him). So if you only trust God and give him a space in your heart, he can assist you in serving him, you cannot do so on your own. Jesus is the only way! The world we are living in today is not on easy one to face. Sometimes we face with a lot of different problems, others trying to destroy others for whatever they need. They do not even stop to think about others how they feel or whatever they need. Those are some of the things that can cause pain within your heart. I have experience those things, and the love of God help me through. Showing the love of Jesus Christ in your heart is very important. As soon as you become a child of God it's very important for you to stick closer to the word of God. I have experience suffering until I know that I was a prophetess send from God. To keep God will and to do his work, I have to be very close to his words! I have been almost approximately locked away from family and friends to know the true and living God. There is times when I have to be alone and at peace so that God's love and his mercy can abide with me. God said if his prophet's should do any thing wrong are leads his people in the wrong direction they will be punish by him. Therefore to avoid any punishment from God, you have to follow his law, which are the Ten Commandments. As soon as you are acquainted with our Lord Jesus Christ, you have to have a lot of faith in Jesus. God send his prophet's into the world so his people can distinguish him through them. A prophet has to know God through Jesus Christ and his Holy Spirit. He or she may have to suffer through many different trials, to recognize that Jesus was the one who leading them. The power of evil has attracted me in many different ways, and God has helped me to over come, through his son Jesus Christ and his Holy Spirit. I have gone three days with pure water and vitamin to have the power of Jesus with me that I could manage through difficult times. And now I come to distinguish Jesus and his Holy Spirit, I would like to tell others all about his wonderful love. If you immediately learn to trust Jesus he will be of assistance to you in knowing he is real. Satan people will be always trying to frustrate you to perform things in their way. However when you have the love of God in your hearts, he will take you out of all danger. I have seen evil ones circled me just like Daniel in the lion den, and God take me away from them unhurt. Jesus is the great you to know him too. He cares for you, he just desire you to come to him as you are, and with an open heart. As soon as you find Jesus, be ye true to him, praised him always, and follows his commandments. When the evil one fighting against you? God will always give you on angel to guide you! I have proved Jesus to be a healer and adviser. Just give him space in your heart, he will here your cry and answer. I can tell you if I did not give him space in my heart I would not able to manage. Jesus is reel!

CHAPTER 9

WHEN I CAME TO THE U.S.A, I HAVE NEW EXPERIENCE, AS IF I WAS IN SCHOOL

When I start having difficult times the vision came to my attention again. I always love Jesus and want to follow his words. There is sometimes you are around the wrong environments and get caught up in the things of the world. You will be distracted from the most important things in your life. I have on experience! Of which prove to me that the Ten Commandments is true and should be kept. I would never eat any thing that my mother taught me not to eat. I was invited to a Christmas party at a friend house, and they had pork in the dinner. I told them I never eat pork because I was taught not to eat it by my mother. They told me to try a little part of it, I did taste it. It tasted good, but I did not want it, because I know it was unclean, and not good for my body. I did not approve it because I know my mother said it was not good for me. The Ten Commandments say we should honor our mother and father, to obey parents is a part of God's rules, it was in me to do what my parents says, so it help me to obey God's rules, which is the Ten Commandments. I have to give God thanks, and give God the glory, to give me the opportunity to know him and want to serve him to the end. I would like every one who read this book to yield to God's calling. God start showing him self to me at on early age, but I still did not know what he was showing me. Now I realized that is one of his ways which he was proving to me that he his true and living God. Jesus can prove him self to you in many diffident ways. It was just for me to open my heart to Jesus and say yes to his calling, and he would help me to know him more. The 16th of January 1993, I had another vision, after I woke up and think about it, I know God can work in mysterious ways and wonder to perform. In the vision I was standing near to the sea with two babies, I was about to take them for lunch. I saw a big mountain, on the mountain I saw a grate big boll cover with net rolling very fast going down into the sea. I ask what that was, and some one says, that was a war booth. The vision symbolized that God can put on end to all things that is not right. The ball that was going down into the sea was a war booth, and that's the way the war came to on end. We are in this world working for different things, and God can wipe out in a twinkling of on eye. Try to serve the Lord now, and put away war from your hearts. It's very important that you do so! Jesus is the answer to all problems. When you really know Jesus, you will love him and serve him, he can make you happy if you let him in you hearts. Some times you will not have money, and you will be happy in your hearts. Matthew 5: 3-8 says! Blessed are they that mourn for they shall be comforted. Blessed are they which hunger and thirst after righteousness for they shall be filled. Blessed are they that meek for they shall inherit the earth. Blessed are the peace makers for they shall be called the children of God. God need us to be at peace, so we can know him, and served. He sends his son to die for us all, so we may follow his foot step. Its takes me 43 years to really know him and love him the way he wants me to love him. I give him praised, and thank to give me the opportunity to know him. So I would like you to give him a chance to help you to know him. My visions always give me a sign. And this one is telling me that we need to stop warring about the problems of this world and think more about our Souls salvation, we need to put all war at the bottom of the sea, and go to Jesus and ask him to help us with any problems. He can give you peace, love, and comfort. Only trust and obey him! Jesus our savoir is sure he is the only one who can give peace in your heart. He cares for you all. You have to do his will, try to know him! By praying, and reading his words, and try to love him. I love Jesus, and I read his words, and pray for understanding and knowledge, that's the reason I can tell you that Jesus love you and that he cares. And he desires all of us to know him. Just give him your heart, he will open it and let you know him, and love him. When you are having a problem? Sometimes you should turn to the Lord for help in ever way, you should ask him to come into your hearts, and help you to know him and also ask him to help you with your problems. Sometimes that's the time we learn to really know Jesus. He love's you just the same. He is a merciful God. He always desire to help you when you in need. Jeremiah 9; 24, tell you that him that glorieth glory in this, that he understandeth and knoweth me, that I am the Lord which exercise loving-kindness, Judgment, and righteousness in the earth. For in these things I delight, saith the Lord. When you give your heart to Jesus he takes care of all your needs. Never get weary he will help you to do his will. When I give my heart to him, I gave it to him so I could work for him and serve him. I have seen work that needed to be done, that I could not even think of my self. I could only found my self thinking about was helping God's people. It was not on easy job, but I always prayed and ask Jesus to help me to do what he wants me to do. Sometimes you will be working with the people and you found them difficult to work with, all you need to do is go to the higher help through prayer. I have done it and found help. So never give up on our Lord Jesus Christ, he will help you as soon as you go to him. Before I accepted Jesus as my personal savior from sin, it was not easy for me to do so. I was told to accept Jesus from on early age, but there was a problem, I did not really know Jesus, therefore I choose to know him on my own. God has chosen a special way, how to train me to know him. Jesus has placed a special child in my womb; as a result he could work through his angel, and let me know him. And it really works. When I was carrying that baby I used to be very careful in what I eat or drink. I did not use any strong drink; I would eat all the things that I know was good for my health. After taking up Baptism! I come to realize his true work. God is a grate and mighty one; he can do many things to prove himself to you. Only trust him, he will find a way to prove himself to you. Let him know you love him and you will always love him and never leave him. He can work miracles and wonders. Jesus is the answer to all your problems if you only trust him. To know Jesus personal for yourself! You have to first believe in him. Love him and trust him. You also have to have faith in him. You can only have those through our Lord and Savior Jesus Christ. After having experience of Jesus order, you cannot run away from him, he will find you were ever you are.

Jesus loves you always, never run away from him.

CHAPTER 10

EXPERIENCE I HAD BEFORE I WAS BAPTIZED

always prayed and ask the good Lord of heaven to help me that when I got baptize, I would do it with him, so I would never turn away from him. I am very happy that it does happen. I have baptized and I am very happy to know Jesus! And to know he give me the strength, to keep to his words. He is very wonderful to me. I can tell you this, to make that step for the Lord is not on easy one. So when you do so, you should always pray to the Lord for help to keep you there in his present, through reading his words and praying always. Because you can not do so on your own. You will always face with trial and temptation. Just have faith in God, and believe in him, and he will help you to do so, he has done it for me and I know he will do it for you. I was born a child of God from birth, because I did not understand Jesus at on early age, that's the reason why he proves himself to me, through a new born baby. I am praying that God will help me to help her to know Jesus at on early age. Jesus can help you in many different ways, if you only trust him. Luke 1: 41-80, tell you that. When Elisabeth heard the salutation of Mary, the baby leaped in her womb; and Elisabeth was filled with the Holy Ghost. When you conceive with on angel of the lord in your womb, you of to depend on the Lord to take you through to the end. The baby I was carrying I had different experience of which I learn more about the Lord. Jonah was disobedience to God order, and God has to prove to him that he can not run away from him. Jonah 1: 2: 3: 4: When he want you to do his will he will prove to you that he rules over you. Jonah was scared and run away you can be filled with the Holy Ghost, and the Lord will Lead you where he want you to go. God is merciful and great in his work. In Jeremiah 1:5-8, said! Before you formed I formed thee in thy belly I know thee, and before thou comest forth out of the womb! I sanctified thee, and ordained thee a Prophets unto the Nations. To tell the world his wonderful news, God is your answer to all your needs. As you come to know Jesus, you will always need him, he is a sure God. I love him and I know you will love him too. Only trust him. Jonah went away on a ship. Thinking he would be safe. The sea got ruff and all the people on the ship got scared, the people spoke to Jonah and ask what we must do? Jonah told the men they should through him out of the ship into the water. The people did just as Jonah told them to do. And after they did that the sea was calm. God was so merciful he let a fish slowed Jonah and God heard his prayer and answer by saving Jonah. Jonah promise that he would do as Jesus told him to do. God spoke to Jonah the second time to see if he would obey Jesus order, Jonah obeyed Jesus order, and he went right away, and he do just as Jesus desire him to do. God knows us all and want us to do his will. // He will let us do it in any way possible. I have experience difficult times which help me to know Jesus. So that's why I would like you to try and know Jesus before it's too late. Jesus loves us all and he wants us to listen to calling. God can speak to you through a servant of God or even from a stranger, also a book, even a letter, and a new born baby. You should always love him so you can see his message; they come in many different forms. Jesus is wonderful! Sometimes you may be scared to do what he want you to do, don't run away, only ask him to help you. He will give you the power to do his work. I have proven him to be true and I know you can prove him too. Just give him a space in you heart and he will help you. Jesus knows you even better than you do know yourself. He knows how you feel, he knows how you think, Jesus, is the only one that can help you to make that right decision. When you think of going to Jesus through baptize, just turn to him in prayer and ask him to direct your part. He will here you and help you, because he first love you. He always gives you a free choice to make your decision. When you get that opportunity you should appreciate it and always try to know God. Jesus wants us to know him. When I was a young girl growing up I always see my mother sending me to a Poster home sometimes. She also let me take voice of prophecy lesson. I came to realized that my mother only needed a little help from the Posters. God has many different ways in training his Prophets. A Poster always need a Prophet help and a prophet always need a Poster's help, A prophet also need a teachers help also a Doctor help. According to God words we should all work together through Jesus love and prayer. So we can work through all things in Jesus name. That the reason why I told my son who is training to be a Poster in collage to let God leads the way. And he must follow, God will help him to do his will and help him to get a good wife, and to archive a good wife or a good husband you have to pray and ask the God through Jesus Christ to help you to make that right decision. This is a very important experience I would like to share with my readers. To know Jesus is much heard when you do not love him, you must first love him to know him. When you come to know him it is even hoarder to keep him. "You will even have more difficult trial and temptation than before; you take him as your savior". As he help you to overcome through bad times. Never give upon Jesus! When you become a child of God? The first thing you should try to do is to be true, be honest, be kind, and loving to others, it's very important. 11 Corinthian 5: 17-18 Tell you that, therefore if any man be in Christ he is a new creature; old things are passed away; behold all things are become new. And all things are of God, who hath reconciled us to himself, by Jesus Christ, and hath given to us the ministry of reconciliation. That's the only way God spirit can dwell in your heart. When you have Jesus, every thing is possible, Jesus care for you always, you only have to trust him, and learn to obey his will. If you follow the Ten Commandments you can not be in the wrong direction. The Ten Commandments is taken from Exodus 20: 1-17 Jesus Laws should be carried out. It's just like living in a country and when the Government passes a law for the Nation to follow and it has to carry out. Jesus Laws can help you to carry out your Governments law. If you love Jesus, you will carry out his Laws. It may seem heard, but all you have to do is love Jesus and trust him. Try to serve him always he will never leave you are for sake you. And as soon as you know Jesus, always help others to know him. Be honest and true when you are training others. God will love you always, and guide you. Jesus needs us to always come to him for what ever we need. He will always here and answers prayer. Give your heart to him in prayer for your needs. Let him feel your need and understand your prayer. It may seems like your prayer did not answer, never give up keep on praying. God answer prayer in mysterious and wonders to perform. 11Chronicles 6: 34-35 tell you that, if the people go out to war against their enemies, then pray unto thee, then will he here your prayer from heaven, and their supplication, and he will maintain their cause. He is always waiting just to here your prayer, and to help you with your needs. Sometimes you can be very Lonely and unhappy, and Jesus come in his way of comforting you. Jesus is always there for you, he cares for us all. I have another vision! And after I woke up from my sleep, I have to sit and think for a moment, It's seems so reel, I also make's me very happy. This is one of my visions which is similar to the vision I had before, it was lighting and thunder flashing, and there was some beautiful angels with lots of bright beautiful stars behind them, they made me very happy. Just to speak about the vision. From what I have seen! It's telling me that Jesus is very near, he will soon to come. I have to share this vision with my readers. I do hope when they read it they will get some help from it, and they will think more about Jesus, and his soon coming. Jesus need us to be ready for his coming, so that when he burst the clouds of heaven we will be happy the way I was when I see those angels. Jesus is the answer to our needs and happiness, we should try to know him and serve him. I have a daughter which is 6 years old, and when I told her about my vision, she was happy also. And she told me write away mammy write that vision in your book. So you see even a child can feel Jesus love. It's wonderful to know that Jesus can make some one happy through a vision. I would like every one to learn to love Jesus and try to know him. He is wonderful! In my lesson study the following morning I found the words in the Bible, 2 Thessalonians 1:7-9 Tell's me the same thing I dream, and to you who are troubled rest with us, when the Lord Jesus shall be revealed from heaven with his mighty angels. In flaming fire taking vengeance on them that know not God and that obey not the gospel of our Lord Jesus Christ. Who shall be punished with everlasting destruction from the presence of the Lord, and from the glory of his power? Jesus is coming soon, and the only way to be happy when he comes, we have to try to serve him now. It's very important, he needs us all to know him and serve him. It's not easy but we must try to love Jesus first. He cares for us all.

CHAPTER 11

MAKING MY OWN DECISION THROUGH GOD

My daughter at the age at 6 years old was telling me what she would like to be when she grew up. She told me she would like to be a Doctor. I would like ever one to know that even a child can make his or her decision. And they can keep them through God, if you guide them in the right way. She also said she want to be a writer when she grew up. When I was able to make my own decision, I always try to do the things that are right in the sight of God. It's nice if every one tries to know the true and living God for them self, before they accept him as there personal savior from sin. Jesus needs you to know him, and be very responsible, so that when you accept him, you will be able to have faith in him, to keep you through good times and bad times. He is the only one that can keep you close to him, let him into your heart, and pray always. He will here and answers prayer. Love's plays a very important part in God's work, also trust. You must first love him and pray and ask him to guide you through you, and ask him to help you to have faith in him. To depend on Jesus is very important! I was able to make my own decision, when I accept the Lord as my personal savior from sin. I choose the Lord and savior as I come to know it was the right way, and I learn of him and know him, therefore I could be able to be close to him. It was very important to me. With out you been able to make that choice on your own? It would be hopeless. Therefore as you come to know Jesus and choose him as your personal savior from sin, you will have joy. His holy angels are with you, and if you choose Jesus, he will help you to know him. 1 Corinthians 1: 27-31 said! But God hath chosen the foolish things of the world to confound the wise; and God hath chosen the weak things of the world to confound the things which are mighty. And base things of the world, and things which are despised, hath God chosen, yea and things which are net, to bring to naught things that are; that no flesh should glory in his presence. But of him are ye in Christ Jesus, who of God is made unto us wisdom, and redemption: that according as it is written, he that glorieth, let him glory in the Lord. Consequently as you can see from this scripture reading, Jesus made choices of his own. So we as human bean should be able to make choices of our own through Jesus. He is our savior! Let him in.

CHAPTER 12

THERE IS A LOT OF DIFFERENT THINGS JESUS IS AGINST

When we come to know the Lord! We should first keep a loving heart. We should judge not, leave all judgments to God! We should love one another, and help others to serve him. These are some of the things that Jesus would not like for us to do. Jesus is against all lying and judging others, and much more. To know Jesus is not very easy, but when you love him, and trust him, you will have faith in him. When I see what I have gone through to know that is the true and living God that is with me. I know that to have faith in the Lord is very important. Sometimes I feel like giving up, and do other thing that is much easer to do, but when I see there is no way, but Jesus way, to true life, love and happiness. It gives me great pleasure to believe in Jesus and have faith in him. He told me that he die on the cross for us all, as a result that we may be save from our sins. Therefore that's why I come to have faith in him, and turn my life over to him. He leads the way for me; the way of the cross and his resurrection is the only way for me. I suffer the way of the cross alone, until a child was given to me, the burden become lighter. So when it comes to mind to give up, I turn it over to Jesus, by following his words carefully, as a result he could lead the way. He gives me strength to go on, and he said I should never give up. Jesus is the answer to all my problems. You can give up and material things, but you can not give up on saving your life. Every one would like to keep their lives; therefore I will fight to keep it. So you see Jesus know just how to get through to you, if he needs you to do his will. His servants can not hide from him, he knows how to find them and keep them. I have to leave mother and father, brothers and sisters and my children to know the things that Jesus need me to do, so I could do his will. I was around strangers, people who did not know me, and God used his miracles to help me to know he was the true and living God, who is with me, and need me to serve him. "I was convicted with out any question." God know that his people is ever were, and he knows how to find them. All we have to do is pray always, and ask him to lead the way. He always here and answer prayer. I grew to love him and want to serve him to the end. And I would like every one to try to know him too. He is wonderful! We who already know him, we should always try to show love to every one in side the church, and out side the church. Jesus love is pure, loving and kind. I have to tell you a little more about my self. And the bad experience I had before I accept God as my personal savior from sin. I used to work much harder, 16 hours per day. I have to cut my hair off, so I could be able to manage to get some rest after I come home from work at 2am in the morning. I was too tired to role my hair. So I put a curl in my hair so I could go to bed after I got a shower. I got 4 hour of sleep and got back up at 6am in the morning to start another job. I done it for about 1year, I could not wake up one morning; I could only pick up the phone and call my boss and quit the morning job. I kept the after noon job, because I could manager better with that paycheck. After a few months at the job I kept, I was told one night that they were going out of business. So I was out of a job for about 2 weeks. I went and look another job; I got the Job the same day. I have to give God thanks God for providing for me. I start working for the company, and after a few years, I start seeing things while I was working at my desk. I speak of some of things I have seeing, and I start worrying, I even used to cry and ask my self why all these thing have to happen. I start getting so unhappy at work; I would worry and cry, I would go in my car by my self. I start getting sick, until I have to go to the Doctor and the Doctor send me to hospital for a nervous brake down. I rest for a few days, and I was ok again. Thank God I over come. It was a very heavy stress and scary experience. But after coming to know Jesus! There was no more scary feeling. I could face all problems with God. He gives me strength to manage. I have face situation were I did not know one person can face. God is great, I would like every one to come to know him, and really love and serve him. You can not do it on your own. I used to try to do it on my own, Jesus stop me along the way and show me the way to his kingdom. He said he is the only one that can help me to manage. It was strange, it was a wonderful experience. Jesus is the only way. When you come to know him, and see how he can work through your heart and mind to let you know him. It will be wonderful when you come to know him and love him and serve him, as I do. Jesus loves you all, only try him! To have faith in God you have to love his words, trust in them believed in them and pray always.

CHAPTER 13

KNOWING JESUS THROUGH YOUR LOVE

A pure love is a wonderful thing to experience! Leaving a person who is close to you, are people in general with a pure heart, can help you to know Jesus is reel? When you Shows love to others, when we come to know the Lord! We ought to first maintain a loving heart. We should judge not, leave all judgments to God! We ought to love one another, and help others to serve Jesus. To know Jesus is in your heart, you have to love him. He can allow you not to be very happy or trouble-free, however as soon as you love him, and trust him, you will have experience the different of not loving Jesus and loving him, that's why I can tell you. Sometimes I do not have any money and yet I am happy. Jesus can help you to know him. I have gone through that experience, that's the reason I can help others to know Jesus. I have been like a baby who needed a mothers care, to know Jesus. It was freighting, but after you really come to know that Jesus can do miracles, you will ///love him and want to serve him. When you love Jesus, then open your heart to him, he will work through you and help you to know him, as a result you can tell others about his wonderful love. Jesus cares and he desires for you to know him and love him. There are times when you will face with difficult people, which you find it hard to deal with. Also difficult trial of life, and you will even ask your self this question, is there a true God? Why these things happening to me? These things that are happening to you are trial and testing of your love and faith in God. Ephesians 6: 10-11 Tell's you that you should be strong in the Lord, and in the power of his might. You should put on the whole amour of God that ye may be able to stand against the whiles of the devil. Therefore you can see all you need when there is trial and temptation come your way is Jesus. Just have faith in him; he is greater than the devil. Jesus can help you to love him and have faith in him. When I see what I have gone through to know that he is the true and living God that has bin with me. I know having faith in the Lord, is very important. Sometimes I feel like giving up, and do other thing that is much easer to do; nevertheless I see there is no way, other than Jesus way, to true life, love and happiness. It gives me great pleasure in the direction of believe in Jesus and having faith in him. He told me that he die on the cross for each and every one, as a result we may save from sins. Therefore that's why I come to have faith in him, and turn my life over to him through his words and prayer. He leads the way for me; the way of the cross and his resurrection is the only way for me. I suffer the way of the cross alone, until a child was given to me that could make the burden lighter. Consequently when it comes to mind to give up, I turn it over to Jesus, as a result he could lead the way for me. He gives me strength to exit, and he said I should never give up. Jesus is the answer to all my problems. You can give up on material things, but you can not give up on saving your life. Every one will like to keep their lives; therefore they will fight to keep it. As a result you see Jesus know just how to get through to you, if he needs you to accomplish his will. Fighting for your life one will work hard and do what ever the LORD wishes for you to do. His servants can not hide from him, he knows how to find them and keep them. I have to leave mother and father, brothers and sisters and my children to know the things that Jesus need me to accomplish, and as a result I could perform his will. I was around strangers, people who did not acquainted with me, and God used his miracles to assist me to know he was the true and living God, who is with me, and require me to serve him. "I was convicted with out any question." God know that his people is ever were, and he being familiar with how to locate them. All we have to do is pray constantly, and ask him to lead the way for you. He for eternity here and answer prayer as you desire! I grew to love Jesus and desire to serve him to the end. And I would like every one to make an effort to know him too. He is wonderful! We who already know him, we ought to constantly endeavor in the direction of showing love to every one inside the church, and outside the church. Jesus love is pure, loving and kind. I have to tell you a little more about myself. And the terrible experience I had before I accept God as my personal savior from sin. I used to work 16 hours per day. I have to cut my hair off; as a result I may possibly be able to manage in the direction of getting some rest after I come home from work at 2am in the morning. I was too exhausted to put rollers in my hair. Therefore I put a curl in my hair as a result I may perhaps go to bed and get some sleep after I got a shower. I got 4 hour of sleep and got back up at 6am in the morning to start another job. I work two jobs for about 1year, I could not wake up one morning; I could only pick up the phone and call my boss and quit the morning job. I kept the after noon job, because I could manager better with that paycheck. After a few months at the job I kept, I was told one night that they were going out of business. Therefore I was out of a job for about 2 weeks. I went and look another job; I got the Job the same day. I have to give God thanks. I start working for the company, and after a few years, I start seeing things while I was working at my desk. I speak of some of things I have seeing, and I start worrying, I even used to cry and ask my self why all these thing have to happen to me. I start getting so unhappy at work; I would worry and cry, I would go in my car by my self. I start getting sick, until I have to go to the Doctor and the Doctor send me to hospital for a nervous brake down. I rest for a few days, and I was ok again. Thank God I over come. It was a very serious stress and terrifying experience. However after coming to know Jesus! There was no more terrifying feeling. I could face all problems with God. He gives me strength to deal with my problems. I have face situation were I did not know one person can face. God is great, I would like every one to come to know him, and actually love and serve him. You can not accomplish knowing Jesus on your own. I used to attempt in the direction of performing the toss on my own, Jesus stop me along the way and illustrate to me the way in which I should follow him. He said he is the only solitary with the purpose of showing me the way to manage. It was strange, but was a wonderful experience. Jesus is the only way. When you come to know him, and see how he can work through your heart and mind to allow you know him. It will be wonderful when you come to know him and love him and serve him, as I do. Jesus loves you all; only make an effort to follow him! To have faith in God you have to love his words, trust in them be lived in them and pray constantly.

Knowing Jesus Through Your Love!

A pure love is a wonderful thing to experience!

Allow somebody to distinguish that you love others, Jesus will be in your heart, and he desires us to love others as we love our selves. Jesus will let you extremely cheerful. I have experience it, that's why I can tell you that Jesus loves you uncondisitional. Sometimes I have no money and yet I am cheerful. Jesus can help you to discern him. I have pass through that experience, that's the reason I can be of assistance in the direction of assistance others to know Jesus. I have been approximate like a baby who needed a mother to care for her, to know Jesus. It was freighting! However subsequent to actually come to distinguish that Jesus be capable of performing miracles, you will love him and desire to serve him. As soon as you love Jesus, subsequently unlock your heart and let him in, he will work through you with his Holy angels and assist you to discern him. As a result you can enlighten others concerning his wonderful love. Jesus cares and he wishes you to discern him and love him. There are times when you will face with difficult inhabitants, which you may find it difficult to deal with. Also difficult trial of life and you will ask your self this question, is there a true God? Why these things happening to me? These things that are happening to you are trial and testing of your love and faith in God. Ephesians 6: 10-11 Tell's you that you should be strong in the Lord, and in the power of his might. You should put on the whole amour of God that ye may be able to stand against the whiles of the devil. Therefore you can see all you need when there is trial and temptation through your love for Jesus. Just have faith in him; he is greater than the devil. Jesus can be of assistance to you toward loving him, and over come any difficulties.

CHAPTER 14

GOD CAN DO THINGS FOR YOU, AT THE RIGHT TIME! AND THE RIGHT PLACE!

There is a very important experience; I would like to share with my readers, to show how wonderful God can do perform miracles for you. When I came to America I have put out great effort working in different jobs, just to take care of my bills, and family back home. It was so heard to do difficult jobs in the direction of performing some jobs you did not even know any thing about, but however God open my mind and heart, and give me the knowledge to perform my work well after I was trained. When you are down and out and you know not what to do, give him your heart, he will help you through all bad times. Just love Jesus, he cares. When you get anger you acquire antagonism and violent, Satan will obtain control of your heart, allows Jesus within you with peace and love, and he will permit you to have happiness. Sometimes even yet the words you speak from your mouth will let Satan to enter in. Endeavor to use Christ like words, Satan can not over power Jesus words. If you used his words he will move you through them, and he will dwell in your heart and make things better for you. If you used Jesus words he will be in your heart always, because you need him. He gives you a free choice to choose him or Satan. Therefore the way to choose him is through his words! Jesus executes the things he asks you to accomplish by speaking his words and pray always, and ask Jesus to assist you to perform what he asks. Jesus is the only solitary one can assist you to accomplish his will. Jesus desires each and every one of us to be like little children, before he can leads us to his throne of grace. Being like a child, is just being humble and patient, kind and loving. 1 John 3: 17, 18, Tell's you that! Who so hate this world's good, and seeth his brother have need, and shutteth up his bowels of compassion from him, how dwelleth the love of God in him. He went on to say! My little children let us not love in words, neither tongue, but in deed and truth. As soon as you have Jesus in your heart and feel like a little child who is in need of training, Jesus will be willing to here you and come to your assistance. Jesus desires you to first open your heart to him as if you really require him to be of assistance you. I know he is wonderful! Therefore I would like you to prove him too at the right time and the right place.

CHAPTER 15

THE TEN COMMANDMENTS IS A LAW THAT GOD ASK US TO FOLLOW IN THE BIBLE

The entire Bible is based on the Ten Commandments. That's God's Holy laws! We are living in a world, of which the Government has a law, for all human bean to follow. If we as human bean would first reflect that we come into this world through our Lord Jesus Christ? And we ought to endeavor to follow his laws; we would be able to follow the laws of our lands or country's. The Ten Commandments is found in the book of Exodus 20: 1-18, Jesus asking us to obey and observe his will. Jesus is the one who give us life existence and he can take it! First love Jesus, be devoted to your self and then continue to loves Jesus who made us. Loving him for even creating you and allow you to come into this world and give you a chance to live, is a wonderful thing to do. He deserves our praised. If you think it's hard to keep his the Ten Commandments? Just reflect of what Jesus did for you, by dying on the cross for each and every one. Jesus said we ought to follow his foot step; we should try making an effort to follow his laws. Sometimes we will have difficult times in doing some things, but we must first remember that Jesus bore more for us. Seeing the importance to follow the law of God, I pray always. Just take it as a partaker of the symbol of Jesus suffering and testing of our faith, these things allow us toward having stronger faith in our Lord and savior Jesus Christ. Sometimes God can use a servant of God to help you to obey his laws. Make an effort to know Jesus through praying! Pray and ask him to assist you to obey him and others as well who can assist you. As soon as they tell you about the words of God and you accept. Jesus will here and answers your prayer always. He never failed. "That's the approach he needs us to follow in the direction of following him!" Jesus is the way, the truth, and the life. "Jesus is coming soon!" We ought to ask him now to assist us. He got peace; he got love for every one. The Ten Commandments is the way to life every lasting life. James 2; 10-13 said! For whosoever shall keep the whole law, and yet offend in one point, he is guilty of all. For he that said, Do not commit adultery, said also Do not kill, Now if thou commit no adultery, yet if thou kill, thou art become a transgressor of the law. So speak ye, and so do, as they that shall be judged by the law of liberty. For he shall have judgment without mercy, that hath showed no mercy; and rejoiceth against judgment. If you should break one point of God commandments and keep the others you are guilty of all. We should follow them carefully and ask God to help us to follow the law of our Land. 11 John 2: 4 tell you that if you say you know him and keepeth not his Commandments he is a liar and the truth is not in him. Jesus is coming soon endeavor to love him and served him.

CHAPTER 16
THE ANGEL OF THE LORD CAME TO ME IN GOD MIRCLES WORK

When the Angel of the Lord came to me, I was in trouble and needed help. God found me and open my heart and mind in the direction of following him, it was so wonderful to know him and accept his calling. The burden and trials was too much in me to carry, my tears were flowing too much. Jesus will find you if you just open your heart even a little to him, I constantly cry to him and ask him to assist me in the direction of knowing his words. As Jesus come to you he will give permission toward you getting to know him, and you will love him and always desire to serve him. The angel that came was the angel that minister to my heart, and gives me the courage to discern him and accept him. I know the same way he assist me assist me in knowing him; he can execute the same for you. Jesus cares for us all, he just desire us to open our hearts to him. When you know his love and understanding that he can give all you need, you will find peace that passes all understanding. The angel just wishes for you to allow him in as a result he can perform his master will. Jesus angel will come to you any were you are! No matter where you are. Jesus knows you all, if you need him and would like to follow him. "Pray always. We all are week, and need his strength." All we need to do is go to him with a pure heart and ask him to be of assistance to you to know the direction of knowing him. "Jesus is always there for you." He is patiently waiting for you to open your heart. As soon as you are ready for the Lord to be in your heart he will send his angel and fill you with his love. He has all the peace and love to fill you with. Mal. 4: 5-6 Tell's you that! Behold, I will send you Elijah the Prophet before the coming of the great and dreadful day of the Lord: And he shall turn the heart of the fathers to the children, and the heart of the children to the fathers, lest I come and smite the earth with a curse. Jesus needs us to open our hearts to him, as a result that when that grate day shall come, you will able to hold fast to him. Have faith in God! He will help you before that grate day of the Lord. You will be able to run to him on that grate day, and not run away from him. When the angel of the Lord came to you, he will open your heart and mind, and give you a free sprit to

62

accept his wonderful words. As you accept his angel and give him your heart to him. He will help you always. Jesus loves us all and only need us to give our hearts to him. I have experience the angels take my life over and lead me through. I have driven through the angel of the Lord. It's a wonderful experience, a very peaceful one. I would like every one to experience those wonderful moments. The only way for you to experience those wonderful moments, is just for you to open your heart to Jesus and let him in. We are in the end of time! It's time we should all open our hearts to our Lord and savior Jesus Christ, our soon coming King. The signs we are seeing today should help us to draw closure to our Lord and savior Jesus Christ. I heard on the news some time in October of 1993, there was a preacher who clams he was disturb by the Government, and he killed his members. God is true! He told us in his words that we should not kill! He never said we should kill others because we were disturbed. When you speak of Jesus wonderful love and his words, we should not add to them or take off from them. God ask us to follow his words. These are signs of God coming and we should prepare the way, with his true words. When you tell others about Jesus, speak Jesus with truth, as a result he can dwell in our hearts. Now is the time for all of us to follow God's words carefully. Sometimes it's seems a great deal to execute God's will. However I would like to tell you! Give your heart to the Lord, and ask him to help you to face trial and tribulation. As a result as soon as problems approach your way, you will never give up! Hold faster to the Lord Jesus, and lay all trial and burden at the feet of Jesus He will take it all from you, and let your heart rejoice for him. Jesus cares very much for each and every one. I have gone through trial and tribulation, and as soon as I go to Jesus with an open heart, he set my heart free from all burden. God work in many different ways! You can even talk with some one who God can work through; he can help you through another person. God can give that person the knowledge to advise you what he wishes you to discern of him. Prayer is the key to our Lord and savior Jesus Christ. Constantly pray! God's here and answer prayer. I can enlighten the world about how much difficulties I have gone through so much trial and tribulation, its hurts so bad inside that I could not do any thing to stop the pain, but turn to Jesus in prayer. As soon as I turn to him I found love, peace, happiness, and he help me to be of assistance to others in the direction of having faith in him, and keep my tears from flowing. I wrote the book because I would like others to know that there is a God that healed all broken hearts. I know you can prove him too, just have faith in Jesus.

CHAPTER 17

IMPORTANT EXPERIENCE THAT I WOULD LIKE TO SHERE

There is one important part in my life experience I would like to share with my readers. When I decided to leave my family and live in the United State, I was planning to make a better life for my family. But while I was planning, I did not know God was planning for me to do his will. He let me have some of the things I always wanted in life, he show me the way to success in life. Then he stops me along the way, and told me to find him. I think of what was happen, it was so hard on me. I used to cry always, wondering why me? And how I am going to manage? And when I see how he learns me to know him while I work, sleep, drive, and eat. God is wonderful! I come to know him, and for me to do what he wants me to do, it become a joy in my heart. I have left my home and family, and know God! And then he began to show me my family again, with open eyes. He promises me that as I do his will, he will take care of me, and I believe he will do so. I would like every one to know Jesus Christ as I do. You have to go through trial and temptation some times. To really believe that there is a savior! Reading about Jesus, and knowing him, is a wonderful experience. Jesus needs us all to know him, and come to him with on open heart. Have faith in Jesus and love him always. Pray always for strength, he will here your prayer will answer, at the right time and place. Jesus cares! God has is means and ways to keep his servants. I always have faith and believe in him. I know he can help you just the way he do for me.

Jesus people is ever were, he said! Some day he will gather them into one place. Because of my faith in him he found me and has me doing his will. Therefore I would like you all to have faith in Jesus always. When disadvantage come your way? He will take you out of it all, no matter how hard the task may be, Jesus here and answer prayer. God love you and so do I. The experience can be a massage from God. "Don't worry! Only pray always! Jesus cares."

CHAPTER 18

FIGHTING AGAINST GOD SERVANTS

There is a very important experience! I would like to share with my readers. I am a child that was born with God love, and his spirit. I have gone through trial and tribulation to realize that Jesus is with me, and need to lead me to do his will. The devil is always there seeking to overpower God servants, but I really come to know that when you love the Lord, there is nothing the devil can do to get God people to follow his way. I was in the world of sin, but yet I always ask him to guide me through ever thing I do, or say. He always guides me, and I come to know Jesus and he brought me to him. And told me that now is the acceptable time for me to do his will. I did not have any choice I have to say yes to him. So I would like ever one who read this massage, to try and love the Lord, have faith in him, believe in him, and pray always. He will find you any were you are. He cares, and so do I. When the devil is fighting against you to overpower you, always remember that Jesus love you, and he is always there as you needed him he is just a prayer away. Jesus said you should call on him always, he will here and answer prayer. The devil will fight you even when you say yes to Jesus, and accept him as your personal savoir from sin. But always remember God is a mighty God, and he never failed, you just have to call and he will answer. Jesus said in his words, you should never be afraid, only trust in him, and have faith.11 Corinthians 7: 5-7 Said! For, when we were come into Macedonia, our flesh had no rest, but we were troubled on every side; without were fighting, within were fears. Nevertheless God, that comforted us by the coming of Titus; And not by his coming only, but by the consolation wherewith he was comforted in you, when he told us your earnest desire, your mourning, your fervent mind toward me; so that I rejoiced the more. As you read these words of scripture, you can see there is a comforter that you can depend on, only go to him in earnest prayer, and he will come unto you. Also 1 Peter 3: 14 Said! But and if ye suffer for righteousness sake, happy are ye: and be not afraid of their terror, neither be troubled. Jesus is with you. Keep him in earnest prayer always.

CHAPTER 19

SHOWING LOVE TO ALL PEOPLE! AND HONOURING MOTHER'S, AND FATHER'S, THROUGH JESUS LOVE

Commencing the day you began to recognize yourself, you should show love to each and every one of God creatures. Showing love to each and every one is very important. As soon as you show love to each and every one, Jesus will rejoice! A day will approach when you will require some one in the direction of showing love to you! As a result I am asking each and every one to show love through God's words! "It's wonderful." When difficult times approach your way? And there is some one to say, this person always love every one, and I will help him or her through his love for others. I come to discern the Lord and to recognize that loving the Lord is very important. When men on earth turn their backs on you? God will for eternity love you. Jesus said! We must love him, trust him, and serve him. If we can find it in our hearts to perform as Jesus asks, in return Jesus will allow us to maintain his love, and accomplish his will. I have come to be acquainted with the Lord as my personal savior from sin, and seen the different from being a sinner. If I did not have Jesus in my heart despite the fact that I was in the world of sin, I would not able to over come sin, for that reason I could have faith in knowing that Jesus is the answer to overcoming all sin. He guides me through his love, that he has place in my heart. If you are a sinner, and not yet given your heart to the Lord? Just love him constantly, and always ask him to assist you to come to him, through praying always, in the morning when you rise, pray, before you go to bed at night, pray, in the car or walking pray, Jesus here and answer prayer. If you do not let him in your heart, Satan will have the power over your heart, the heart is a part in your body that can be desperately wicked if you let Satan in it. Jeremiah 17: 9, 10 Said! The heart is deceitful above all things, and desperately wicked: who can know it. I am the Lord search the heart I try reins, even to give ever man according to the fruit of his doings. 11 Thess.1: 7, 8, Tell's you that, and to you who are trouble you rest with us, when the Lord Jesus shall revealed from heaven with his mighty angels. In flaming fire taking vengeance on them that know not God, and that obey not the gospel of our Lord Jesus Christ. Being with Jesus before he comes it's very important. Jesus said he is coming soon with mighty Angels, with flaming fire to take vengeance on them that know him not him Jesus. I am asking every one that read this book that they will, take these words as a massage from God servant, and make an effort to love Jesus and accept his calling, before it's too late! Jesus is pleading to us to come to him now, he love's each and every one of us with on everlasting love. 1 Samuel 16: 7 Said! But the Lord said unto Samuel, Look not on his countenance, or on the height of his stature; because I have refused him for the Lord seeth; for man looketh on the outward appearance, but the Lord looketh on the heart. At what time he comes! We all would like to meet him. If we don't accept his calling now, we will here, depart from me I know you not. I am sure no one would like to here Jesus said those words to them. Jesus loves us all and wants us to just open your heart to him, and ask him to help us, to come to him. Reading this massage will help you to accept God calling and ask him to help you to come to him. Jesus experience is a wonderful one, as you come to know him; he cares and loves us all! Make an effort for Jesus.

CHAPTER 20

TRIAL AND TRIBULATION! AFTER ACCEPTING THE LORD AS MY PERSONAL SAVIOR FROM SIN!

Subsequent to becoming a child of God! That's the time trial and tribulation began. You should for eternity look toward Jesus for that special help and guidance, in the direction of keeping you close to him. We are living among other people in the world of sin, and we need Jesus strength constantly to overcome trial and tribulation. It's very important at what time you say yes to Jesus, you should constantly depend on him through reading his words and prayer, and keep him in your heart and mind always. Without his assistance to keep you close to him it's imposable. Jesus desires you to depend on him always. Satan will be constantly trying to acquire you back out into the world of sin, to carry out his will. However you ought to first remember that you made a covenant with your Lord and savior Jesus Christ, who is the maker and keeper of all things. Jesus can help you to resist the devil at all times. Constantly read your Bible, pray always, and asking Jesus for understanding, as a result he will be able to work through your mind and heart to lead you. You must always have faith in Jesus, believe in him forever. Some times life will seems to become even difficult than before you accept the Lord, and you will began to think why life is not easer than before? These are some of the trial and temptation you will face, subsequent to becoming a child of God. Don't ever give up! Turn to Jesus even more in prayer. He promises that he would provide for his children. He is sure! 2 Corinthians 1: 19, 20 Tell's you that! For the son of God, Jesus Christ, who was preached among you by us, even by me and Silvanus and Timotheus, was not yea and nay, but in him was yea. For all the promises of God in him are yea, and in him Amen, unto the glory of God by us. John 14: 1-3 Tell's you that: Let not your heart be troubled: Ye believe in God believe also in me. In my father house are many mansions: If it wore not so, I would have told you. And if I go and prepare a place for you I will come again, and receive you unto myself;

that where I am, there ye may be also. Ye believe in God believe also in me. He said! In my father's house are many mansions, he gone to prepare a place for us and he will come again and receive you unto myself. Therefore no matter how hard things may seems with you, don't give up! Have faith in God. He loves you with unconditional love, and so do I.

CHAPTER 21

DISCOVERING HOW GREAT GOD CAN BE

When you discover God greatness! And how wonderful he is, you will never desire to ever leave him. He is really a miracle working God. As soon as Jesus work miracle in your life and prove to you that he is the son of God, you will love him additional forever. Jesus can prove to you how great he is, by assisting you to overcome difficult times. If you just let Jesus in your life? You will know him. I have discovered his wonderful work with the accomplishment of a new born baby, and it gives me joy to magnify his name forever. He can work miracle in many different ways, I would like every one to make an effort to discover Jesus in their lives, and just give him a chance to prove him-self in your heart and mind. I needed to knows so much from I was a young girl, and all though I attended school and Church, I still did not know the right thing that Jesus desire me to know, until I was about 41 years of age when I finally say yes to his calling. Jesus bring me to a standstill along the way, I could not go to work for a period of time, I have seeing Jesus in many different ways, through his written words, and through visions, and through the great things I have seeing he grew in nature, nevertheless as soon as I come to really discern him clearly that's the time I take up baptism on my own free will, and decided to follow him as my personal savior from sin. I was baptize at the age of 12 years of age, but I was back in the world of sin because of my first child. He open my eyes to each and every test that he used to perform in me, and show me that he live within me, and he care's for me and require me to accomplish his strength of character. I grew to love my Lord very much. And promise to never leave him and that I will perform his will accordingly. Discovering Jesus is one of the most wonderful things could ever happen to any human bean. He gives me a chance to choose for myself and to gain knowledge of things of the world I am living in today, as a result when I say yes to him there will be no turning back. "Jesus is reel." Try and discover him in your life, as I accomplish knowing

Jesus, by letting him in your heart and mind constantly, through reading his words and praying always. Jesus will direct the way for you! He cares for you all. He said in his words, he will make you white as snow. You can be clean as if you never commit any sin. Isn't that wonderful, trust God and follow his words, Jesus love's you with on everlasting love.

CHAPTER 22

WHEN YOU KNOW JESUS AND LOVE HIM! YOU WILL KNOW HOW MUCH YOU CAN HAVE FAITH IN HIM?

As it comes to the close of another year, and I realize that I am alone and still happy to know that I can hold fast to Jesus and feel joy in my heart, its make me exceptionally happy toward knowing that as soon as you put your trust in Jesus he will guide you through trying times. I have so much bad experience during 1993, and if I did not have faith in Jesus, I would be back in the world filled with sin. I can offer thanks to God and praise to keep me and care for me. I do hope every one can discover the identical faith in God, for that reason that at what time, bad times faces them they can overcome with joy flowing over their hearts, through Jesus. On the 12-31-93 I was saying to my 6 year old daughter that I am third of being alone, and I am hoping for a better 1994. She came to me and hug me and said to me mammy you are not alone I am with you. I hold her and kiss her with a smile and said I know you are with me. Again I was joyful in my heart. Jesus is the solitary that maintain us faithful to him, and have us joyful by our self. I know he can do it for any one who trust in him and love him. These are sometimes in our lives that we need to prove Jesus. He's the answer to all our problems. We only need to establish faith in him, and trust him.

CHAPTER 23

OVERCOMING STRUGELLING TIMES THROUGH GOD'S LOVE

At what time you say yes to the Lord and savior with a sincere heart? He will guide you through; I have answer to Jesus our soon coming king! And I am rejoicing in him today. When I say yes to Jesus through baptism, I was going through difficult times. And God told me he his the only way to overcome the difficult times I was facing, I was going through financial problem and loneliness'. I have seeing difficulties in my life of which I think I would never overcome. I can see where God is showing me the light and he have taking me out of a condition of which was very difficult, and I recognize that he is the risen savior. And I know he will do more if I only keep on trusting in him. I would like every one to have that faith in him as I do. He is a wonderful savior! Who never failed? You only have to put your trust in him and never give up. He cares! He only wants you to say yes to him with all your heart. Jesus is the only over comer for us every single problems. Let him lift you up from all your problems as he done for me, Problems will come upon you, but never give upon Jesus. You are his children and he cares for you all. Revelation 3: 21 Said! To him that overcome will I grant to sit with me on my throne, even as I also overcome, am set down with my father in his throne. As you study God's words, and pray Constance for Jesus to be of assistance toward overcoming difficult times, Jesus will here your prayer and answer. Trust in the Lord and be strong in him.

CHAPTER 24

JESUS IS THE SAVIOR! HE WILL LEAD YOU, IF YOU LET HIM IN

J esus cares for us so much that he dies on the cruel cross for us. We may be suffering on earth, but Jesus suffers more for us all. His father could have stop all that he was going through. The pain, the spear in his side, the nail in his hands, God want us to know that he done all so we can come to know him through his son Jesus Christ. Jesus wants us all to know him before he comes, so he sends Jesus to save us. We are in the end of time! The things we are see happing around us today; we can see that Jesus is nearer at the door. He is pleading to all, through many different ways and things, for us to accept him and follow him. It may seems difficult to accept Jesus, If you just turn to him with all your heart and ask him to lead you through all that you need to know, he his willing to help you. Isaiah 41: 10 said! You should fear thou not for I am with thee, be not dismayed; for I am thy God: I will strengthen thee, yea I will help thee, yea I will uphold thee with thy right hand of my righteousness. Jesus just needs us to open our hearts to him and he will lead you through all things. Philippians 3: 9-12 Tell's you that, and be found in him not having mine own righteousness, which is of the law, but that which is through the faith of Christ, the righteousness which is of God by faith, that ye may know him and the power of his resurrection, and the fellowship of his suffering, being made comfortable unto his death.

If by any means I might attain unto the resurrection of the dead. Not as though I had already attained, either were already perfect: but follow after, If that I may apprehended that for which also of Christ Jesus. So you see from reading this scripture, it tell you that! To know Jesus and his resurrection, and attained his perfect love, you can be sure. Jesus need's us to know him! If a person is honest and loving, the one who discovers these qualities never seems to feel that he or she knows enough about that person. When that person is your creators and savior and feel desire to know Jesus better. You will know no limits. This experience and desire to know Jesus better is the result of a genuine one and righteousness by faith. Knowing Jesus! Means allowing him in your lives through God grace. Gal. 2:20 Tell's you that I am crucified with Christ, nevertheless I live: yet not I but Christ liveth in me: and the life which I now live in the flesh "I live by faith of the son of God, who loved me, and gave himself for me. Jesus now lives in us, it's just for us to seek him and know him, and he will reveled himself to us all. Have faith in Jesus Christ our soon coming king! He is reel, and soon to come. Jesus gives us a free choice to choose him or Satan. We have to learn to make choices of our own. Jesus is a willing savior! He will not push you unless he see it nursery to be done, if he see in you a willing heart to learn of him, then he will prove himself to you in any way he need's to do so. Jesus is reel! Try and find him through his words, he loves us all.

CHAPTER 25

DANGER THAT IS UNBERABLE AND ONLY THE LORD COULD HELP!

I have seeing danger for a period of over thirteen years. And in attendance was no solitary to turn in the direction of other than the Lord and savior Jesus Christ. We are in a world of sin, the people we are around ever day they are changeable, they are unbearable, they treat one another as we don't recognize that there is a good Lord above. Jesus cares concerning each and every one, he is asking for us to make an effort and be acquainted with him and follow him, he is a wonderful God, and we need to make an effort to have a heart like Jesus. He has born the pain on the cross for us, and still he loves us until the end of time. We ought to first love Jesus as a result we can love others. Fighting one another for different reason, of which do not facilitate our hearts to love God. God be capable of changing things for each and ever one. I could remember when I was younger and having my children, I had a visitor came to my house and while we were talking, he ask me what I would do if I have to leave my house and go away, and another woman take over? What would I do? My answer was I would not let that happen, because I suffer and work too heard to leave my home after I made it to another woman. But little do I know that while I was planning God was wiping it out, therefore I could discern him and perform his will. God has plan for me commencing the time I was conceive. He never leaves me or for sake me. He only gives me time to be acquainted with what he can execute. I have learned from my experience that I should allow God to make plans for me. God changes things! He can perform it for you, if you let him in your hearts. I let him in my hearts, that's why he could change my thinking. John 10: 18 Tell's you that Jesus has power to lay it down and power to take it up again, he said no man take it from him, because he has got that power and commandment from his father. When we say to our self, I will not make things happen; we should always end our saying by using these words, if our Lord and savior Jesus Christ permit me accomplish what ever we need to perform in life? Or let me have it. He is the great God! And we should learn to trust him, and obey him constantly. Jesus can stop all difficulties or problems.

CHAPTER 26

"BE READY!" FOR THE LORD JESUS IS SAYING TO US, WE NEED TO BE READY FOR THE COMING OF OUR LORD AND SAVIOR JESUS CHRIST!

Jesus is at our door! As we can see the things that has been happening around us today, in this world that we are in, you can learn from them and see clearly that the Bible is fulfilling. Jesus needs us to answer his calling now! Because the time is near! When he comes and you are prepared to meet him, you will be joyful to witness him, burst the clouds of heaven. And not running to the mountain and be afraid. When you are ready there will be no fare. You will only have joy to behold him. Jesus can give you the heart to face him face to face with out any fare. Each and every one of us need to accomplish, is on the way to be ready through his words. Only obey him as he asks. He cares for each and ever one and desires us to be ready for his kingdom. Jesus is pleading to us in many different ways. He gives us signs through the heavy rain each year. He gives us sun shine that is unbearably. He gives us the winds that blow the trees down, and a great deal more. We should acquire time to serve him, since he his great and mighty in our sight. Jesus is near and at the door! Let's serve him now.

CHAPTER 27

MASSAGE FROM GOD!

When God has a messenger he used them in many different ways, one technique can be through writing a book, another approach can be through a person, and another method can through payer. God love his people and pleading to them to come to know him in many different conduct. Jesus has been trying to discover his creature in every way. Jesus said we should answer to his voice now! He is at hand. He has been using me from I was a child, until I come to discern him, as a result I possibly will deliver his massage. I promise that I will here his voice accordingly; I am telling every one to make on effort to be aquatinted with Jesus through his wonderful words, and license to his servants, in what ever way they comes to you that are the right method. Jesus is pleading to us to come to him and follow him, as he has followed his father's foot step. "Jesus father and the Holy Spirit is our only savior." Jeremiah 31: 10, 11 Tell's you that Jesus desire us to here his words! He said! Here the words of the Lord, O ye nations, and say he that scattered Israel will gather him, and keep him as a shepherd doth his flock. For the Lord hath redeemed Jacob and ransomed him from the hand of him that was stranger than he. With those wonderful words that Jesus our savior gave to us, we need to recognize him and serve him. Jesus can be of assistance to you, if you just allow him to understand your requirements, he cares for us all, even when we sin against his commandments, give permission to him to enter into your hearts and he will assist you to discern him. Jesus messengers are very important people! You ought to here them now.

CHAPTER 28

SATAN FIGHTING AGAINST GOD SERVANTS!

disappear from the world of sin! And say yes to Jesus through baptism. In attendance I realized there is people that is in the world of sin demanding to get a hold of me to come back to the sinful world; they would try in every possible way to show me that I have to perform things in their approach. However because I come to discern Jesus, and promises to serve him through to eternity, he gives me the strength and faith to avoid the world of sin and those people. I am praying for them all, and that the eyes of everyone will release to Jesus before it's too late. Jesus is the only solitary that can save you from sin. He will give you the strength and faith to believe in him; as a result you can be saved in his kingdom. He loves us all! Jesus only desires to be acquainted with your love for Jesus as your personal from sin. The simply way for any one to prove his or her love for Jesus, is through accepting Jesus words, and say yes to him through baptism. Satan will be constantly there trying to overthrow God's people, even when you say yes to Jesus, you will discover that he will used ever possible trick to try to get you to come his way. To overcome that struggle you should put Jesus first in every thing you do are say. Speaking Jesus is a very important part of getting strength from our Lord and savior. You will find that Satan flee from your heart! Let Jesus in with all your heart. He will take care of you. Colossians 4: 1-6 Tell's you that Master give unto your servants that which is just and equal. Continue in prayer and watch in the same with thanks given, with all praying also for us that God would open unto us a door of utterance to speak the mystery of Christ, for which I am also in bands, that I may make it manifest as I ought to speak. He also said walk in wisdom, toward them that are without redeeming the time, let your speech be always with grace, seasoned with salt; that ye may know how ye ought to answer every man. Jesus is saying that you should be ready, so that when Satan people try to win you to their way, he will give you strength through words, that you speak, even the things you do, Jesus can help you to overcome any difficult times you may faces! Have faith in God and pray until the end of time. Jesus cares for us each and every one.

CHAPTER 29

CRUSIFIED WITHOUT BEING NAILED TO THE CROSS!

Present was nothing left to achieve other than battle for my existence through the authority of God. I accept God calling, it was the correct timing, God needed me to execute his self-control; I did not refuse to accept answering to his calling. It was during my suffering, there was so much to execute for him that all I could do was to go to him in prayer. I prayed several times per day for him to guide me and he did. All I could see around me was danger, and God rescued me from all danger and put me on my way rejoicing. I could remember when I was young my mother would like me to be a child of God, and I always say yes in my heart, but I did not say yes to Jesus publicly. And when the day come that I say yes to Jesus it was just in time to work for Jesus, a mother and father is God guidance for his children, we should endeavor to follow them carefully, when they are following Jesus words. My mother is always putting God first in her life. That's the reason when I was being crucified on the cross she always come to my rescued. Jesus is our only hope; he can speak through you if you allow him in your heart. He has given me understanding and knowledge, so I could over come. Jesus cares; you should give permission in your hearts. He will be of assistance to you through all dreadful times, Jesus has been crucified for us, and as a result he will not let us nail to the cross, because he has boor it all for us when he nailed to the cross. Nevertheless you can be crucified in performance and deed. Make an effort to seek Jesus before it's too late! Jesus is coming soon.

PROVING JESUS THROUGH SUFFERING AND SHARING HIS LOVE TO OTHERS!

At what time you have gone through long suffering and draw closer to discern Jesus as your personal savior from sin, we should always share what we gain knowledge of, with others. Jesus has special conduct in reaching out in the direction of his people. He has stopped me along the way; as a result I could discern him. And he desires me to help others to be acquainted with him. Jesus is reel! He wishes you presently to say yes to him and he will open your eyes to things you never knew. Some times when you are suffering, turn to Jesus with your old heart and request him to be of assistance to you in the direction of understand why your life is difficulties or why you are suffering? Jesus will answer your prayer, and he will be of assistance to you toward discerning him. Do not go to Jesus without being sincere in hearts and mind, open your mind and allow him in, he recognize that you require his assistance; He will not turn you away. Jesus just desires to give us a free choice to come to recognize him, as a result that is why he is so patient to his people. Jesus could lead us without asking us to follow his words. However that's not the way his father requests him to perform his strength of character. God love us each and every one, however he desires every one to require him in our lives, and come to him through his commandments. God given us a law in his Holy Bible and he desire us to follow him, that's his method of letting us recognize that he his giving us a choice. You have to go through difficult times sometimes to be familiar with the Lord. He can give you all that you need. Just put all your trust in him, and there will be nothing he will not accomplish for you. Constantly endeavor and put Jesus first. He loves you and concern for you. You can be suffering because Jesus need you to be a special servant for him, and he had to lead you in any way he chouse to accomplish your action. You know Jesus is reel. Philippians 3: 9-10 Tell's you that we are found in him, not having mine own righteousness, which is of the law, but that which is through the faith of Christ, the righteousness which is of God by faith.

That I may know him and the power of his resurrection and the fellowship of his suffering being made comfortable unto his death. John 10: 18 tell you that no man takeeth it from me. He said but I have lay it down of my self, I have power to take it up again this commandment have I received of my father. Therefore as you read these scripture you can see what Jesus can accomplish through his father. Jesus gives you life and he can take it from you. We should all make an effort to discern Jesus and say yes to him, so he can speak to you, and open your eyes to come to be acquainted with him. Jesus is the only way! Jesus said as soon as you come to recognize him and follow him; he will come and receive you with him into his kingdom. Jesus said! All his promise of God is yea and in him amen. He also said! He will seal us, and gives us earnest spirit in our hearts. 11 Corinthians 1: 20, 22, said! Jesus knows our hearts, where there is a problem that we can not deal with he is willing to assist us, he can change our hearts to a heart of love and peace. If we just say yes to Jesus. He loves rejoice. I am proving him now even more than before. I have seeing my baby daughter Kimberly says yes to Jesus at the age of 7 years of age. I could remember my other children always constantly asking me for baptism at on early age, I always tell them they were too young. I come to realize that God was calling them at on early age too. I say yes to Kimberly at the age of 7 because I just come to discern the Lord, and distinguish what he can do in our lives early or older. He his wonderful, he can take care of you no matter how young you may be. Andrea and Mervin accept God at on early age too, they are two of my children, and God is taking care of them too, he also takes them through collage. Jesus is wonderful, only trust him. Matthew 17: 20 Tell's you that, If ye have faith as a grain of mustard seed, ye shall say unto this mountain, Remove hence to yonder place ; and it shall be remove; and nothing shall be impossible unto you. Have faith in God, always. He cares for you all. So you need to be acquainted with him before it's too late. When a child is born of natural birth, through suffering it's not on easy pain to bear. The child that comes from a mother whom through a knife, that's a pain that is unbearable, only Jesus know. Sometimes these things happened to prove to us that the pain Jesus bears for us. Jesus desires us to be familiar with him, and he will let us discern him in any way he discovers possible to be of assistance to us toward discern him. Jesus said we should search for him and endeavor to recognize him. It's not on easy way to distinguish that Jesus life, however sometimes these are some of the conduct to assist in bearing the cross of Jesus. The child can be a special symbol to assist you to discern Jesus. Therefore we should make an effort to be acquainted with Jesus in any way he desires us to recognize him. Jesus cares for us each and every one. Isaiah 11: 1-3 Tell's us that there shall come forth a rod out of the stem of Jesse, and branch shall grew out of his roots, and the spirit of the Lord shall rest upon him, the spirit of wisdom and understanding, the spirit of counsel, the spirit of knowledge and of fear of the Lord. And shall make him of quick understanding in the fear of the Lord, and he shall not judge after the hearing of his eyes. Subsequently you can see in support of you to be acquainted with

God words, he will prove himself to you and give you quick understanding. We need to know Jesus for our self; as a result he can help us. Jesus is of assistance to me in the direction of knowing him through pain and suffering, I know he can allow you discern him as well. Trust him and fear him he loves you with on everlasting love, and he desired for you to be save in his kingdom.

CHAPTER 30

JESUS IS THE KEY TO ALL THE HEARTS THAT NEED TO BE OPEN!

When you have gone through long suffering and come to know Jesus as your personal savior from sin, we should always share what we learn with others. Jesus has special ways in reaching out to his people. He has stopped me along the way, so I could know him. And he needs me to help others to know him. He is reel! He want's you just to say yes to him and he will open your eyes to things you never knew. Some times when you are suffering, turn to Jesus with your hold heart and ask him to help you to understand why your life is difficulties. He will answer your prayer, and he will help you to know him. Do not go to Jesus without being sincere hearts, open your mind and let him in, he know you need his help; He will not turn you away. Jesus just wants to give us a free choice to come to know him, so that is why he is so patient to his people. Jesus could lead us with out us asking him to follow his words. But that's not the way his father wants him to do his will. God love us all, but he needs us all to need him, and come to him through his commandments. He given us a law in his holy Bible and he want us to follow him, that's his way of letting us know that he his giving us a choice. You have to go through difficult times sometimes to know the Lord. He can give you all that you need. Just put all your trust in him, and there will be nothing he will not do for you. Always try and put Jesus first. He loves you and care for you. You can be suffering because Jesus need you to be a special servant for him, and he had to lead you in any way he chouse to do. You know he is reel. Philippians 3: 9-10 Tell's you that we are found in him, not having mine own righteousness, which is of the law, but that which is through the faith of Christ the righteousness which is of God by faith, that I may know him and the power of his resurrection, and the fellowship of his suffering, being made comfortable unto his death. John 10: 18 tell you that no man takeeth it from me. But I have lay it down of my self, I have power to take it up again this commandment have I received of my father. So as you read the scripture you can see what Jesus can do through his father. Jesus can give you life and he can take it from you. We should all try to know Jesus and say yes to him, so he can speak to you, and open your eyes to come to know him. Jesus is the only way! Jesus said when you come to know him and follow him; he will come and take you with him to his kingdom. Jesus said! All his promise of God is yea and in him amen. He also said! He will seal us, and gives us earnest spirit in our hearts. 11 Corinthians 1: 20, 22, said! Jesus knows our hearts, where there is a problem that we can not deal with he is willing to help us, he can change our hearts to a heart of love and peace. If we just say yes to him. He loves us all. I am proving him now even more than before. I have seeing my baby daughter Kimberly says yes to Jesus at the age of 7 years of age. I could remember my other children always asking me for baptism at on early age, I always tell them they were too young. I come to realize that God was calling them at on early age. I say yes to Kimberly at the age of 7 because I just come to know the Lord, and know what he can do. He his wonderful, he can take care of you no matter how young you may be. Andrea and Mervin accept God at on early age too, they are two of my children, and God is taking care of them too, he also takes them through collage. Jesus is wonderful, only trust him. Matthew 17: 20 Tell's you that, If ye have faith as a grain of mustard seed, ye shall say unto this mountain, Remove hence to yonder place ; and it shall be remove; and nothing shall be impossible unto you. Have faith in God, always. He cares for you all. So you need to know him before it too late. When a child is born of natural birth, through suffering it's not on easy pain to bear. The child that comes from a mother whom through a knife, that's a pain that is unbearable, only Jesus knows. Some times these things happened to prove to us that the pain Jesus bears for us. Jesus needs us to know him, and he will let us know him in any way he find possible to help us to know him. Jesus said we should search for him and try to know him. It's not on easy way to know that Jesus lives, but some times these are some of the ways to help to bear the cross of Jesus. The child can be a special symbol to help you to know Jesus. So we should try to know Jesus in any way he want's us to know him. Jesus cares for us all. Isaiah 11: 1-3 Tell's us that there shall come forth a rod out of the stem of Jesse, and branch shall grew out of his roots, and the spirit of the Lord shall rest upon him, the spirit of wisdom and understanding, the spirit of counsel, the spirit of knowledge and of fear of the Lord. And shall make him of quick understanding in the fear of the Lord, and he shall not judge after the hearing of his eyes. So you can see for you to know God words, he will prove him self to you and give you quick understanding. We need to know Jesus for our self, so he can help us. Jesus helps me to know him through pain and suffering, I know he can let you know him too. Trust him and fear him.

CHAPTER 31

JESUS IS THE KEY TO ALL THE HEARTS THAT NEED TO BE OPEN!

You just need to say yes to Jesus through baptism. Some times it's so heard for a person to open their hearts to Jesus, because we have so many problems in our lives. Jesus said! If we just come to him as we are? He can open our hearts to love him and know him. When you come to know Jesus and love him, your heart will be open with such wonderful feeling; you will not even worry about the problems of life. Just pray with your heart and tell Jesus all your problems. He can take them away and give you a new heart. I have gone through trial and tribulation to know Jesus and to know that he can give you anew heart. If I did not love the Lord and know him, I could not go to him in prayer with my problems and prove him. When I go to him in prayer he give me peace of mind, he give me love and joy in my heart. I know he can do the same for you too. He cares for us all. 1 Peter 5: 6 Tell's you that, you should humble your selves, therefore under the mighty hands of God, that he may exalt you in due time. From this scripture reading you can see all Jesus would like you do is to humble your self and let him in your heart. I have seeing the light of the Lord our soon coming king, and when I see trial faces me I turn to the Lord in prayer, and he give me piece and love within and more faith to hold faster to his wonderful words. You will find some friends and family who will try to show you that giving your heart to Jesus in not right, they will try to show you things of the world, but when you come to know the Lord for your self, no one can change you from loving Jesus. Jesus is the only way. I have gone through it all and still I will not give up. Sometimes you will even become a child of God through baptism, and in your church, you will find even your own breading or brothers and sisters not showing you the love of God! Don't ever get weary! It's better for you to stay home even for a few days and be in quite place with your Lord and you, by praying with out ceasing or you can visit other churches and meet other brothers and sisters. Never give up on your Bible, it's the only way. Jesus cares for us all! He wants us to be faithful to him always. Jesus can give you the peace within your heart that can help you to stand, be ready continually, and guard you from danger and insult; we shall not take neglect or slightest of heart, we shall deaf to reproach, and blind to scorn, and insult. Jesus can take you through, if you only let him in your and pray always, he will here and answer prayer.

CHAPTER 32
BELIVING IN JESUS SERVANTS IS VERY IMPORTANT

Jesus said! If you can see his servants and believe in them, then you will believe in him when you come to know him. There is a time in our lives when we here the word of God through his servants and we do not yield to their massages. Jesus is pleading to us in many different ways. His servants can be our own brothers or sister that we are seeing every day. Or even a poor person which you meet on the street who will come to you in a very simple way and tell you that Jesus love you and want you to be save in his kingdom. God servants learn his or her work sometimes through suffering. Many of us today, when we are making money and having a good life, we seem to forget who give us the job to make a good life, we should take it into consideration that God can call us when he is speaking to through others. These are some of the reason why God let us go through difficult times. We ought to stop and think for a moment! Who help us to have health, strength, so we can work to get the things we already have, and the things we need. Jesus knows our insides and our lives; he knows who he needs to speak through him to his people. So when you here God massage from any one? You should try to understand and believe in his words. If you do not understand, you should pray to Jesus and ask for understanding, and help to know him. Love Jesus! His servants are special people, it takes time and patients for them to know Jesus lives so they can tell others that Jesus love them. Don't ever believe that there is never a God who cares for you! He care and love us all. We just have to turn our hearts to him and tell him you need his help, and he will always here your prayer and answer. Before I come to know Jesus! I always pray to him and ask him to help me to know him, and always said I would like to know him for my self before I say yes again in baptism. Thank God it did happen and I come to know him and I promise to always serve him. I would like every one to know him for them self so they can say yes to Jesus before they are baptize. When you accept him, and know him, you will always love him and no matter how difficult it may seem, you will always love him and you will never turn away from him. Jesus is the only way, when you know him and trust him always. John 3: 11-12, 18 Tell's you that we speak that we do know and testify that we have seen and ye receive not our witness, he said if I have told you earthly things, and ye believe not, how shall ye believe if I tell you of heavenly things. He also said he that believeth on him is not condemned but he that believeth not is condemned already, because he hath not believed in the name of the only begotten son of God. Jesus is reel! Love him and trust in his mighty words.

CHAPTER 33
BELIVING IN GOD LAW!

T he Ten Commandments should be treated with respect! When you become a true believer of God law? We should always believe in it and respectful about God words.

When we covet one another, it's a sin in the sight of God. When you begin to covet, you will begin to think wrong, and do wrong things that are not right to others. We should always love one another, so that we will always think good things about others. Being a child of God, and a law abiding keeper is a very important part of God Commandments. Jesus said! If we should do what he asks he is willing to for give us for all our sins. Jesus cares so much for us, so why should we break the Law of God? If we should do God will as he should ask? He will give us strength and a sound mind to do his will, and to keep the Law of our Land or country's. He can give you strength to do well to others. You will always think well about others. And help others not to think of hurting others. Some times we will hurt our friends in a very simple way, and take it for joke. God does not like idle words, he wants you to be loving, kind, caring, and loving one to another.

Exodus 20: 1-18 Tell's you all that God's want's us to do. That's our guide line towards love and caring. If you have the Ten Commandments in your hearts, you will always love others, and never think wrong about others. I speak most about covet, because that's where hurting others come from. When you have coveted in your heart, you can not have love in your heart also. Satan will take control over your heart and speak to you through your heart also, to do the things that are not right to others. Exodus 20:17 Tell's you that you should not covet thy neighbor's house. Thou shall not covet thy neighbor's wife, nor his servants, nor his made servants nor his ox, nor his maid servants nor his ox, nor his ass, nor any thing that is thy neighbor's. If we should follow those words we will always think love in our hearts for others. I have experience others hurting me through my life, and take it as a joke, which is a sin, most of what happening causing them to do so is covet. If I did not have the Ten Commandments in my heart, I would be hurting most of the time, but through prayer and keeping God Law, I do not hate any one. God through his son Jesus Christ can help you to love one another. So you will not think covet so Satan can tell you what to do to others. Jesus is the only one that can help you to keep the Ten Commandments! Just love him and ask him to come into your heart through prayer. God love's you and so do I. Let God help you to respect his Laws, so you will never broke it, when you are a believer of God's Laws, you need his strength to keep them and respect them. If we love them we will respect them and we will never want's to break any of them. If you should broke one and keep the others, you are guilty of all. So put God first in your heart and he will help you to love and keep his Commandments, and respect them. Let him in! He loves you and care for you.

CHAPTER 34

BEING ON TIME TO GO TO HEAVEN!

Jesus is coming soon and he care's for us all, that's the reason why he gives us time to be ready for his second coming. His time is very important; we should always try to be on time for him. It will be too late if we let the hour pass. Jesus will be ready to judge his people when he comes, so we should be ready. Jesus said! We should be prepared, which means we should seek him and find him now, through his holy words. The Bible is the way to find Jesus! While you read his words and understand them, that's the way you will learn what Jesus need you to do. When he comes to judge his people and they are not ready. It will be too late to be prepared. So your soul will be lost. 1Kings 8:61 Tell's you that you should, let your heart therefore be perfect with the Lord our God, to walk in his statues, and to keep his Commandments as at this day. When Jesus said! Let your heart be perfect with the Lord, means you should be ready until the he comes to judge his people. Jesus cares that why he give us time to be ready. He is merciful, caring, loving, and patient. All we need to do is open our hearts and let the savior in. By praying daily and asking the Lord to help yon to know him, he will here you and answer your prayer. Jesus is the only way! Let him in. When you know Jesus! And understand his words, and follow them; you will be ready and waiting to see your Lord and savior Jesus Christ. When life seems hopeless on earth, you will just be joyful, knowing that you are ready to be with the Lord. "You will be telling others how wonderful Jesus is in your heart, and asking them to try and find him, so they can serve hind and be ready as you are. There will be no if and but in your heart thinking that you are not ready, because you know him and are ready to meet him. Joy will be all over your hearts always. He is our savior that's pleading to us to be ready for his second coming. When we are a child, we go to school to be able to read and write, so we can be trained and be ready to take on examination, and be able to pass, and ready to work at any job to make a living. So that's what Jesus is all about, he has given us a period of time so we can be trained to know him and serve him, before he come. He comes before, and he will be coming back again to redeem us! To be ready for his heavenly kingdom to rain with him for ever with his angels, and have no more suffering, no more pain, that will be a glorious day if we are ready. Jesus love's us, because he is a patient's father to us. Read Jesus words, pray every day. And help others to know him as you learn if him. Then you will be ready to meet him in the air. Jesus cares!

CHAPTER 35

JESUS WAS CRUSIFIED ON THE CROSS! WHY DID HE NOT WALK AWAY FROM THE WICKEDS

Jesus is God son; he could save his son from being killed by the wicked ones, on the cross. Jesus did not walk away, because he cares about his people. He gives his life for to save us from our sins. Jesus done all for us so we could have the privilege to know Jesus and over come our sins. His body was beaten, the nail in his hands, the spear in his side. All that was for us, his love for us was unconditional. What would have happen if he had walk away? We would not be able to be saving in God kingdom. So if Jesus can go through all the pain and suffering for us? Why can't we give him a day or anew hours of our time? So he can save us from our sins. He had suffered and dies for us. And all he is asking for is for us to love him and serve him. Jesus cares for us all. We are in the end of time, and he his still pleading to us to come to him through his words. Sometimes we may be suffering! Think for a moment; ask your self why are we suffering? Can this sign be a sign between me and my savior Jesus Christ? He had suffer and die for me and I know he ask us to follow his foot step. This suffering could means that I am severing the wondrous cross as a symbol. Jesus needs you to know him, so he can show you himself in many different ways. Jeremiah 9: 24, 25, Tell's you that Let him that glorieth glory in this that he understandeth and knoweth me, that I am the Lord which exercise loving kindness, judgment, and righteousness, in the earth for in these things I delight, saith the Lord. He went on to say, Behold the day com, saith the Lord, which I will punish all them which are circumcised with uncircumcised. Jesus knows us more than we know our self. He knows what we can do and what we will do. He could have save his self from the cross. But he did not because he wanted to obey his father will. He dies to save his people from their sins. So why not serve him now! He cares for us all and wants us to know him.

CHAPTER 36

BEING LOCK AWAY AS DANIEL IN THE LION DEN! GOD WAS THE ONLY SAVIOR

There is times when life seems hope less! And you feel like you are been lock away in prison. God said! There is a way out. If you only trust him he will save you from all danger. I have seen my life come to a stop, of which I feel like I am at the end of a long rope, and God pull me in and show me the way. When you trust him, he said there is always a way out through him. When God need's you for a purpose? He will find a way to leads you. No matter how heard you may try to do things on your own, Jesus said! Now you are my servant and I must have you to do my work. Never give up! Always trust in Jesus, believe in him, and depend on him always. He is the leader for us all. And he will leads you in what ever way he can. I would like every one to come to know Jesus as I do, and know what he can do. So that we will learn to trust him and do his will. Jesus said! Let him that glorieth glory in this that he understandeth and knoweth me that I am the Lord which exercise loving-kindness, Judgment, and righteousness in the earth. For in these things I delight, saith the Lord. Jeremiah 9: 24 God said! You should not let your faith stand in the wisdom of men, but in the power of God. When you have power from God, through faith in him, you will overcome all things. No matter how hopeless it may seem. Jesus is the answer! Have faith in God always. He cares for us all, and wants us to depend on him. Psalm 91 11- 16 Tell's you that, God will give his angels charges over you to keep thee in all thy ways. Because he hath set his love upon me, therefore will I deliver him; I will set him on high because he hath known my name. He shall call upon me and I will answer him: I will be with him in trouble: I will deliver him and honor him. With long life will I satisfied him and show him my salvation. God has made grate promises to his faithful people, if we obey him and keep his commandments. He cares for us and wants us to know him and follow him. And he will fulfill his promise to all. Jesus said! You must be strong and have courage and he will always help you. No matter how hopeless the case may seem, Jesus can help you. Just put your trust in him and love him always. Jesus said! Therefore if any man be in Christ, he is a new creature; Old thing are passed away; behold all things are become new. 11 Corinthians 5: - 17 Where take unto you the whole armor of God, that ye may be able to withstand in the evil days, and having done all to stand. Eph. 6: 13. As you know Jesus, and love him, and trust him, you will be gone to have faith in him. Faith cometh by hearing, and hearing by the word of God, Romans 10: - 17. Believe in Jesus and he will be always there for you in time of trouble. As you need him he will be there, that's his promise and I know he wills fulfilled his words.

CHAPTER 37

WHEN YOU COME TO KNOW JESUS AND LOVE HIM

Knowing Jesus is very important! As you come to know him you will love him. And he will always make himself know to you in many different ways. You will have trial and temptation comes your way. Jesus will be always there for you to comfort and chair. He cares for us all. The world of sin that we are living in today is not good for any one health. Jesus is the only way to lead us, and help us out of danger. I have come to know Jesus and prove him in so many ways, that I always love him more. He will lead you in every possible way in which he can get you to follow him. That's the way Jesus love are to his people, he loves us uncondisonnelly. All you need to do is let him in. When he said he will be with you always, it's the truth! When you are in trouble, just let him know that you need him in a sincere way in prayer. And always promise him that you will serve him unto the end. He will be with you always and help you in what ever way you need help. He will always help you to serve him! And pray to Jesus always! He love's you and care for s all.

CHAPTER 38

JESUS WAS CRUSIFIED ON THE CROSS! WHY DID HE NOT WALK AWAY FROM THE WICKEDS!

Jesus is God's son; he could save his child from being killed by the wicked ones, on the cross. Jesus did not walk away, for the reason that he cares about his people. He gives his life for each and ever one to save us from our sins. Jesus prepared all for us as a result we may possibly have the privilege in the direction of be acquainted with Jesus and over come our sins. His body was beaten, the nail in his hands, the spear in his side. All that was for us, his love for us was unconditional. What would have happen if he had walk away? We would not be able to be saving in God kingdom. Therefore if Jesus can go through all the pain and suffering for us, why can't we give him a day or an hour of our time? As a result Jesus can save us from our sins. He had suffered and dies for us. And all he is asking for is for us to love him and serve him. Jesus cares for us, each and everyone. We are in the end of time, and he his still pleading to us to come to him through his words. Sometimes we may be suffering! Think for a moment; ask your self why are we suffering? Can this sign be a sign between me and my savior Jesus Christ? He had suffer and die for me and I know he ask us to follow his foot step. This suffering could means that I am severing the wondrous cross as a symbol. Jesus desires you to be acquainted with him; consequently he can show you himself in many different ways. Jeremiah 9: 24, 25, Tell's you that Let him that glorieth glory in this that he understandeth and knoweth me, that I am the Lord which exercise loving kindness, judgment, and righteousness, in the earth for in these things I delight, saith the Lord. He went on to say, Behold the day come, saith the Lord, which I will punish all them which are circumcised with uncircumcised. Jesus knows us more than we know our self. He knows what we can do and what we will do. He could have save his self from the cross. However he did not because he wanted you to obey his father strength of character. He dies to save his people from their sins. Therefore why not serve him now! He cares for us all and desires us to recognize him. 11Thimothy 3: 12 Tell's you that, yea, and all that will live Godly in Christ

Jesus shall suffer persecution. Also Galatians 6: 12 Tell's you that, as many as desire to make a fair show in the flesh, they constrain you to be circumcised; only lest they should suffer persecutions for the cross of Christ. As soon as Jesus desires you to be a servant for him, he will find you! The Bible Tell's you what he will do. As you read these scripture you can see, sometimes suffering can cause from the cross of Jesus. He has gone through suffering for us. Therefore we have to carry the cross as a symbol to be acquainted with Jesus. As you understand Jesus words, immediately endeavor to follow them, and he will acquire the suffering from you. Jesus suffers and dies; as a result he could be rich. "Don't be afraid." Jesus is with you, with all his Holy angels. He will never leave you! The way to salvation is a ruff one! Nevertheless it can be joyful in the conclusion. Thus never give up! Put your trust in Jesus, and pray constantly! Jesus cares.

CHAPTER 39

BEING LOCK AWAY AS DANIEL IN THE LION DEN! GOD WAS THE ONLY SAVIOR

There comes a time when life seems hopeless! And you experience loneless like you are been lock away in penitentiary, and God said! There is a way out; if you only trust him he will save you from all danger. I have seen my life come to a stop, of which I feel like I am at the end of a long rope, and God pull me in and show me the way. As soon as you trust him, he said there is always a way out through him. At what time God need you for a purpose? He will find a way to leads you, no matter how heard you may attempt to perform things on your own, Jesus said! Now you are my servant and I must have you to accomplish my work. Never give up! Always trust in Jesus, believe in him, and depend on him constantly. He is the leader for each and every one. And he will leads you in what ever way he chouse. I would like every one to come to be acquainted with Jesus as I do, and distinguish what he can do. As a result we will gain knowledge of trusting him and perform his will. The Lord said in Jeremiah 9: 24! Let him that glorieth glory in this that he understandeth and knoweth me that I am the Lord which exercise loving-kindness, Judgment, and righteousness in the earth. For in these things I delight, saith the Lord. You should not let your faith stand in the wisdom of men, but in the power of God. When you have power from God, through faith in him, you will overcome all things. No matter how hopeless it may seem. Jesus is the answer! Have faith in God always. He cares for us all, and desires us to depend on him. Psalm 91 11- 16 Tell's you that, God will give his angels charges over you to keep thee in all thy ways. Because he hath set his love upon me, therefore will I deliver him; I will set him on high because he hath known my name. He shall call upon me and I will answer him: I will be with him in trouble: I will deliver him and honor him. With long life will I satisfied him and show him my salvation. God has made great promises to his faithful people, if we obey him and keep his commandments. He cares for us and desires us to be acquainted with him and follow him. And he will fulfill his promise to all. Jesus said! You must be strong and have courage and he will always help you. No matter how hopeless the case may seem, Jesus can be of assistance you. Just put your trust in him and love him always. Jesus said! Therefore if any man is in Christ, he is a new creature; Old thing are passed away; behold all things are become new. 11 Corinthians 5: - 17 wherefore take unto you the whole armor of God that ye may be able to withstand in the evil days, and having done all to stand. Eph. 6: 13. As you discern Jesus, and love him, and trust him, you will begin to have faith in him. Faith cometh by hearing, and hearing by the word of God. Romans 10: - 17. Believe in Jesus and he will be always there for you in time of trouble. As you require him he will be there, that's his promise and I know he wills fulfilled his words.

CHAPTER 40

WHEN YOU COME TO KNOW JESUS AND LOVE HIM!

Knowing Jesus is very important! As you come to know him you will love him. And he will always make himself know to you in many different ways. You will have trial and temptation comes your way. Jesus will be always there for you to comfort and chair. He cares for us all. The world of sin that we are living in today is not good for any one health. Jesus is the only way to lead us, and help us out of danger. I have come to know Jesus and prove him in so many ways, that I always love him more. He will lead you in every possible way in which he can get you to follow him. That's the way Jesus love are to his people, he loves us uncondisonnelly. All you need to accomplish is give Jesus permission into your heart. When he said he will be with you constantly, it's the truth! When you are in trouble, just let him know that you need him in a sincere approach in prayer. And forever promise him that you will serve him unto the end. He will be with you always and help you in what ever way you require help. He will constantly help you to serve him! And pray to Jesus always! He love's you and care for each and every one.

CHAPTER 41

I HAVE SEEN THE POWER OF GOD, AND PROVE HIS STRENGTH.

I have come to know the Lord through difficult times! I have seen his power move in a very great way, and take me out of dangers. Satan has his people who he used to get you to do his will, but through Jesus loves for us, he gives me the faith to overcome. When Satan put you in the Lion den? God can take you out. All he need's you to do is to love him and have faith in him. To achieve that faith you have to depend only on our Lord Jesus Christ! And pray always and ask Jesus to guide you in every ways. When the way seems dark, put your trust in God more, never get weary! It's very important that you love him, and believe in his words. When I was going through difficult times Jesus shows me the way, to overcome. I know he can do the same for you too. He lives within you, if you let him in, he will guide you always. Matthew 17: 20 Tel's you that! Jesus said unto them! Because of your unbelief: for verily I say unto you, if you have faith like a mustard seed, ye shall say unto this mountain removed hence to yonder place. And it shall be removed. And nothing shall be impossible unto you. Having faith is God! It's very important. You can have that faith only through his love; you must love Jesus through his Commandments. He said! If you love me keep my Commandments. If you be obedient to his words, and his holy spirit, he will help you to have faith in him. He cares for us all, so we should try to know him, so he can help us to have faith in him. Marriage is a very important part of one's life if it's done in the rite order. I was married once, and during my thirteen years of marriage, I always never happy about one important part of my marriage. I always ask myself why I did not get a marriage that was more Christ like. I was married to on unbeliever, which was of Christ in his own way, but not a Seventh-day- Adventist. Since I come to know the Lord, I realized why I used to feel that way. God love is true, and I think each one should know Jesus before getting married, so you can know Christ like love.

Jesus love can leads you into true love for your husband or wife. God love is true, and I think each one should know Jesus before getting married, so you can know Christ like love. Jesus love can leads you into true love for your husband or wife. We should try to know Jesus before saying yes to any marriage vows. Jesus loves us all, and want us to have true love so we can know him. Jesus is love! So if we know love we can know Jesus.

CHAPTER 42
THERE IS RULES IN GOD'S HOUSE

In God's house he gives commands for us to carry out! For us to have peace and happiness, we should endeavor to do his will. Our homes on earth should have rules also. Jesus said! We should follow him. When you go to other people homes you will notice that there is rules in their home also we should always try to follow them. We can have peace in our homes just by following rules. When you go to the house of God? There are rules, we should abide by them. If you should go to the house of God and see there are rules for you to follow, and you find it's a problem for you to abide by them, you should leave their homes, as a result we can have peace. Jesus love peace in his house, he want's to be in our homes. So we have to let peace abide in our hearts and our homes. Jesus cares for us all; we just have to let him in. Jesus is love, peace, longsuffering, caring, and merciful. There is a home are various homes that God cannot abide in; because for the reason that we do not give permission him in. If you do the things of the world or things that Satan love, God will not dwell in your homes or your hearts. God gives you a free choice, so; as a result you can invite him in your heart, and home. Jesus want's to illustrate to you love peace and happiness, that's what he have to offer you if you let him in. Jesus said! We should love one another as we love our selves. Sometimes it does not happen that way because we do not have love in our hearts, so we can not give love to others. To have Jesus love in your hearts we must put him first, so we can love others. We have to pray always constantly, for Jesus to help us to do so. 11 Chronicles 6: 34-35 Tell's you that, if thy people go out to war against their enemies by the way that thou shalt send them, and they prayed unto thee toward this city which thou hast chosen and the house which I have built for thy name. Then here thou from the heavens their prayer and their supplication, and maintain their cause. Jesus just want's us to pray to him and ask for help, and he will here your prayer. He can give you peace. Jesus is so reel once you come to know him. A verdict was passed by the law of the U.S.A. curt Judge; it was about a man who was charge for murder. The case has been trying for a very long time; it takes months before the verdict was passed. Jesus verdict can takes sentries, because he is very merciful and patient. I have seen on the 2, 16, 1995 the person that was on trial was not guilty. When the murder took stand, and I heard the news about what was happen to the two people lives, I was anger and would not watch the long trial. I think it was a very wrong thing for any one to do to another person. But between the 15th and the 16th of February I was at school, and the case come to my taught very strong. After leaving the class room, I was on my way to the bus stop to take the bus and go home. And the Holy Spirit told me he was not guilty; I got my note book out and wrote the date down in it. I saw O.J. Simpson on the news and I could not see him guilty, it was 2,16,1995 at 11:45am I see him not guilty. The day the verdict pass I was at school again. Every one was very excited about hearing the news. I sat and I listen very carefully. As they open the letter and about to read the verdict I got up and when I heard the verdict read I only find my self shout and lift my hand and say yes I could not see it in him. I always take a good look at the man on T.V. and I said to my teacher I could not see it in him. God has a way of dealing with us if we let him have a part in our lives. Jesus can help us to do the things that is right, if we just let him in our hearts. We have to try make an effort to let Jesus in our heart, so that when he comes and passing verdict on us, he will be able to say we are not guilty of the wrong things we may done to our friends and neighbors said we do. Jesus is the greatest Judge of all, we immediately need to allow Jesus in our hearts and learn to trust him. Matthew 5: 18,19 Tell's you that, for verily I say unto you till heaven and earth pass, one jot or one title shall in no wise pass from the Law, till all be fulfilled. Whosoever therefore shall break one of these least Commandments, and shall teach men so, he shall be called the least in the kingdom of heaven. But whosoever shall do and teach them the same shall be called great in the kingdom of heaven. (Amen) Jesus loves us all and desires us to serve him. Try making an effort and be acquainted with Jesus and then try to follow him before its too late. Too late will be the cry when Jesus comes and we are not ready.

CHAPTER 43

WHEN JESUS GET'S READY? YOU HAVE TO BE READY!

Jesus our soon coming king is a very patient Lord! He will give us time to get ready for him. The time will come when he will say I am ready for us, and there will be no turning back. That's why he will give us so much time to seek him, and find him. He cares for us all and wants us to need him in all that we do and say. He want's us to let him in our hearts, and that's the way he will be able to manifest his power in us, and give us the strength to serve him. If you just love him and say yes to him by repenting and be baptized and humble yourself to him, he will help you to know that he is reel, and live in every human hearts. If you just open your heart to Jesus alone and do not do the things of the world, so Satan can try to over power the Holy Spirit of God. God will let his son Jesus work, in your hearts and let you love him always. He cares for us all. Luke 12:40 Said! Be ye therefore ready also for the son of man cometh at an hour when ye think not.

CHAPTER 44

TRYING TO SERVE THE LORD, AND OTHERS FIGHTING AGINST YOU!

Y ou can be trying to be making on effort in the direction of being a faithful child of God and others fighting against you, they are trying to get you to go in the direction of perform things their way, and it may seem very difficult for you, some times you may even feel like giving up. You ought to try to believe in God and be faithful and strong in the Lord, as a result that others will not be able to have their own way with you. Jesus can be of assistance you toward being a faithful child of God. He can be of assistance to you in the direction of being strong, you presently have to trust in Jesus and follow his words carefully. As soon as you have Jesus words in your hearts, others will not able to over through you in whichever approach they may take. I have to read Jesus words sometimes to bring relief to my pain, it makes me put all my faith in Jesus, and I become stronger in God. I know that the Bible speak about these things would happen in the end of time! We just have to be in the right order as a result that when he burst the cloud of heaven, we will be ready. I would like every one to take note of the signs of the coming of the Lord. Jesus is very near, that's the reason for all these wickedness that we are facing today. Jesus said! We should get ready before he comes, therefore now is the time for all people to be in the direction of getting ready for the return of our Lord and savior. To be acquainted with Jesus and to be ready you required to follow his words. The Bible Tell's you all you need to discern in the direction of follow his words, and to be ready. John 14: 1-3 Tell's you that, you should let not your heart be trouble ye believe in God believe also in me, in my father house are many mansion. If it were not so I would have told you, I go to prepare a place for you and I will come again and received you unto my self, that where I am there ye may be also. Ephesians 3: 16-17 also Tell's you that, he would grant you according to the riches of his glory, to be strengthened with might by his spirit in the inner man. That Christ may dwell in your heart by faith; that ye being rooted and grounded in love for Jesus Christ and have faith in him. He will always constantly assist you to be ready in the direction of meeting him when he comes. Presently cast all your trust and care at the feet of Jesus, and follow his words carefully, till he comes! Jesus cares for each and every one. Fighting against the servant of God is wrong in the sight of God! We should endeavor to love every one through Jesus love. It may be difficult to love others when you are hurt by them! However if you love Jesus you will be able to for give and love them even when you are hurt. Jesus is love! And he is the solitary one can be of assistance to you in the direction of loving others. Sometimes the person you are fighting against can be a servant of the living God. They may not treat you nice at all times, nevertheless that do not means he or she do not love you, they may be caught up in heavenly business and unable to do earthly things at that moment. Never fight against others for the reason that they change in different attitude. Jesus some times has to leave his disciples to be at peace with his father. So when he his training his servants he may have them do things in a different way from you. Romans 13: 8 Tell's you that you should owe no man anything, but to love one another: for he that loveth another hath fulfilled the law. Colossian 3: 12-13 said! Put on therefore, as the elect of God, holy and beloved, bowels of mercies, kindness, humbleness of mind, meekness, longsuffering; forbearing one another, and forgiving one another, if any man have a quarrel against any: even as Christ for gave you, so also do ye. You can see from these scripture reading that Jesus is asking us to forgive others and love others. Jesus is love! Love endures all things, Jesus cares.

CHAPTER 45

KNOWING THE LORD, AND REMEMBERING WHEN THE STRUGGLE IS OVER, AND GOD SHINE THE LIGHT OF DELEVEREANCE OVER YOU, WITH JOY AND HAPPENESS!

"Jesus is reel". I can see the light on the 15th of may 1996 when I come to the end of the rope and there was no where to live, no money to obtain a new place, all the money I had was just to pay storage for a month to keep my things and a small amount to rent a place for me and my 9 year old daughter Kimberly for the first week. And I have some help from the Government to buy food. I could not worry, all I keep doing in my heart, is putting the case to our soon coming savior, I take my daughter to school and tell her to have faith in God, and have faith in me. I know that there is a true God that I serve, and I know he cares. He said he will make a way for me. I know out of all the promises to me from friends and relative. God would make one of the doors open for me. The day is not yet finish; therefore I do not give up, the song writer said! Never give up, trust in the lord and take hold. The time is now 11:49am, my things is all pack to up at the home where I now live and weighting to get transportation to go to the storage, as a result I could give up the place. Jesus is the same yesterday today and for every! Therefore I keep having faith and hoping that he will send a messenger to be of assistance to me soon. I have constantly promise the good Lord that I will forever serve him, and when the door of success is open there will be always a part in the direction of accomplishing his work. By letting others know that there is a true and living God that we need to serve, we have to tell them that Jesus lives and you know him. It was 11:55pm when my brother arrives with transportation and takes me to his home with my daughter. I have to give God the praise for his assistance constantly.

CHAPTER 46

WHEN I COME TO KNOW THE LORD, AND SEE THE WORK HE WANT ME TO DO!

I was joyful to discern the Lord, and I really desire to serve him. When I see the work he desires me to perform, I was very nervous! But I did not scare. I turn to Jesus in prayer and fasting, he guide me ever step of the way, like a young child who was guided by a mother. I put my trust in the father son and Holy Ghost. He here and answer my prayers, I become stranger and more pure each day. I felt like a new person. Jesus cares for us all, and he lives! We just have to go to him in prayer; he is waiting to answer you. The work faces me any were I was at home, at work, at Church! Jesus leads the way! I began to praise him joyfully when I go to Church, because I come to prove that he was reel, and true. My heart was always rejoicing when I found Jesus. I come to know that there is a God that's leads. We just have to learn to trust in his words and pray constantly. To be acquainted with Jesus was a very difficult training, I always cry, for the reason that when he open my eyes to things I did not be acquainted with, after coming to know that it was only the true and living God that could win my heart in such a pure way, it brings tears to my eyes. I come to discern Jesus as my personal savior from sin. Therefore I try to hold my tears, and pray supplementary. I always pray 3 to 4 times per day. I found relief and become stronger! My tears were dry up, and I start facing the work that was set before me to accomplish. I depend on Jesus as my leader! There was no one else to depend on, all I could see around me was danger, trouble was every were I turn! I laid it all at the foot of the cross. Jesus cares! He let me know him and I know he will let you know him also, if you just let him into your heart. Job 13: 15, said! Though he slays me, yet will I trust in him: but I will maintain mine own ways before him. Job 39: 11 Said! Wilt thou trust him, because his strength is great? Or wilt thou leave thy labour to him? Proverbs 1: 5 also said! A wise man will here and will increase learning; and a man of understanding; shall attain unto wise counsels: As you read these scripture and see how great our Lord and savior can attain unto us. We need to follow his words and learn to trust and obey them. Jesus loves us all! I have come to know him through suffering; nevertheless it helps me to learn to trust in Jesus, and to depend on his promises. I recognize he is sure and reel. When you come to be acquainted with Jesus? Make an effort to believing in his words, and trust in him. Jesus know when you faces him, you will depend on him and trust in his words. Jesus lives in you! He just wants you to open your heart to him and let him in. He gives us a free choice to choose him. Satan will try to portrait to be like Jesus! But when you come to know him you will overcome, and when you over come Jesus will let you sit on the right side of his throne in his kingdom. Jesus cares! Let him in. I now perform the work he desires me to accomplish with joy! With out him I can do nothing.

CHAPTER 47

TO KNOW THE LORD IS NOT ON EASY THING TO DO!

Sometimes life may change, and you began to experience difficulties or pain, and you may wonder! What is happening to me? Life even began to seem hopeless, at that point some of us may turn to the Lord, some may worry about what happen to them, until you learn what is the problem, you will be confuse. When you get sick, until you go to the Doctor and the Doctor examine you, and notify you what he or she see happen to your body, you will not know! Jesus desires you to be acquainted with him as your personal savior from sin. He has to put you through trial and temptation, and he will train you through his Holy Spirit. There are different spirits, Jesus need you to know the true and righteous spirit. Satan will perform close to be like Jesus spirit, so that's why Jesus wants you to choose as a result that you may know him, which is the true spirit. The Bible says! The word of God is the true spirit. St. John 6: 63 Said! It is the spirit that quickeneth; the flesh profiteth nothing: the words that I speak unto you, they are spirit, and they are life. Also Deuteronomy 8: said! And he humbled thee, and suffered thee to hunger, and fed thee man-na, which thou knewest not, neither did thy father know; that he might make thee know that man doth not live by bread only, but by ever word that proceedeth out of the mouth of the Lord doth man live. Jesus will not lead you any way different from the word of God! He is a true and sure God. Satan is imitating the spirit! He will show you the things which seem true like Jesus, but it is not Jesus way. He will lead you into part that seem right to you, but it will not be right. Jesus will never fail you; he will lead you into all that is right. Joshua 21: 45 said! There failed not aught of any good thing which the Lord had spoken unto the house of Israel: all come to pass. Also Joshua 23: 14 said! And behold, this day I am going the way of all the earth: and ye know in all your hearts and in all your souls, that not one thing hath failed of all the good things which the Lord your God spoke concerning you; all are come to pass unto you, and not one thing failed there of. As you read these scriptures, you can see that Jesus the father son and Holy

Spirit never failed. When the problems come upon you? Just turn to Jesus in prayer and fasting, he here and answer prayer. The trial may just come upon you for a testing of faith in Jesus! As a result you can love him and learn of him. When the sickness come upon your body, is because we are resting God calling, and he need you therefore he have to leave your body and that when Satan will be able to take control of your body, and you will become sick. Your body is the temple of God. 11Corinthians 6: 16 Said! And what agreement hath Christ hath the temple of God with idols? For ye are the temple of living God; as God hath said, I will dwell in them, and I will be their God, and they shall be my people. And Satan can at the present not dwell in there, he will tries, but if you let Jesus in your heart. He will remove all sickness and pain from your body. Jesus father could stop the one son he had from dying on the cross. But he let it happen because he needs him to perform his work. To know Jesus is not on easy thing to accomplish, but if you allow him in your heart and mind through his words, prayer, and fasting, he will let you know him very easy. Jesus presently desire you to have a choice, you must be acquainted with him in the direction of being able to choose him. Jesus cares for each and every one, trust in his words.

CHAPTER 48

JESUS IS LOVE!

Jesus love is pure! He is pure because he is Devine, he is sure, and his love is the fulfillment of God commandments. If you come to love Jesus you will be able to keep his commandments, as he asks us to execute. Jesus love's us! He gave his life for us, so we may be able to be saved in his father's kingdom. Jesus love is everlasting, it never failed. Come to Jesus through his words, fasting and prayer. And you will know him and love him. When I was suffering with out a job, and needed help, I turn to my Bible and pray and fast and he start to show me his love in my heart and mind. Jeremiah 31: 3 Said! The Lord hath appeared of old unto me, saying, yea, I have loved thee with on everlasting love: therefore with loving kindness have I drawn thee. Proverbs 10: 12 also said! Hatred stirreth up strifes: but love covereth all sins. 11Corinthians 13: 11 Said! Finally brethren, farewell. Be perfect, be of good comfort, be of one mind, live in peace; and the God of love and peace; shall be with you. As you read these scriptures you can see that Jesus is love, with out Jesus you can do nothing in his sight. The love of Jesus can leads you through all things, you just have to come to know him and how wonderful he is, if you choose him in your life. Try Jesus love through his words, he cares for each and every one. When you come to know Jesus and his wonderful love for you? You will prove that Jesus is love. Loving Jesus with your heart and mind, you will see that he is pure and devine. Jesus words are life and strength. Learn to depend on his words and his promises. Jesus is love! Trust in him, and believe his words. Jesus love is divine and pure. In the direction of having a life with Jesus love, you have to seek for him, and find him through his words, and acknowledge his words and say yes to him through baptism. The love of Jesus can cleanse you from all unrighteous. Presently learn to trust in Jesus, he loves you each and every one. The love of Jesus can help you to over come all obstacles, his love is great. Put your heart in his hands, he cares for us all. He is Devine and sure! The words of Jesus never failed. Trust in his words and pray until the end of time. Jesus lives in the hearts of each and every one of us if we just let him in, you will find that love for all others, and for Jesus. He can help you to be pure and divine. With out him you can not find that love that is above ever other love. Jesus is love follow his words always.

CHAPTER 49

JESUS IS ALIVE! I HAVE PROVED HIM, IN WAYS THAT IS AMAZING

Yes Jesus is alive! I have proven his matchless name and his love, and how great he is to his people. When you go through the storms, the wind, and the darkness with out any lights in your home, and overcome? You can know that there is a beam that is above ever other beam. Jesus lives! The day I arrived home from work, the sun was very hot. I was burn from the heat; my air condisition was broken in my van. I was in just for a few hours when the wind and the rain began! The place I am living in, all the windows began to flew open, and I began to get confuse, I rush out in the wind, and go to my next door neighbor and ask him to help me clause my windows, he come and help me quick before the heavy wind and rain started. It was very freighting because that was my first experience of seeing a storm; I have seen heavy rain, but not threes blowing to the ground. After the storm pass, we had no light for almost 2 weeks, it was very difficult for me. I had to used candles and a small wormer which used with lighter fluid towards making a meal. I recognize before that happen there was a God! But after seeing all that happen during the storm in our state and others states. I know for sure that there is a God that is alive. Jesus give us signal to allow us distinguish what he can carry out in the direction of showing us what can happen in a moment. We should make an effort in the direction of recognizing that there is a beam that is above ever other beam. He lives! He is merciful, he can destroy us, and he can save us. The wicked things that some people execute on the face of the earth, faces God and he is grieve; he is showing us signs of what he can execute. The word of God is guide line for us, so we can over come difficult times. He lives and he wants us to live also, we have to accept his words and follow them, so we will able to live with him in his father kingdom. Isaiah 38: 16 Said! O Lord, by these things men live, and in all these thing is the life of my spirit: therefore wilt thou recover me; and make me to live. Also John 14:19 Said! Yet a little while, and the world seeth me no more; but ye see me; because I live, ye shall live, also. Therefore as you read these scriptures, you can see that Jesus lives and because he lives we have the privilege of living also. Trust in his words! Live by them in your daily lives, because he is able to help us through his Holy words. Jesus would like us to follow his foot step. He cares for each and every one. And as you come to know Jesus, never leave his present. Prayer and fasting is the key to the heart of Jesus love.

CHAPTER 50

DISADVANTAGES, THAT HAPPEN TO GOD SERVANTS THROUGH LEARING TO KNOW JESUS OUR LORD AND SAVIOR!

The servant of God has gone through great trial and temptation, to be acquainted with Jesus! Toward being acquainted with Jesus, the servant of to be in the direction of being like a child again, during those time I have experience great trouble, for the reason that the people of this world do not understand, or failed to understand that God is using that person in the direction of performing something special for his second coming. Jesus needs his servant to accomplish his will! When an adult be converted into a little child again? It's not on easy obsession for any one to experience! There is a point when you are spoken to or treated like a child, and you know it and have to take it for granted with a smile, that's not easy! You recognize that this is disadvantage, and you may not like it at that time and you have to allow it pass for the reason that Jesus is testing your faith. Yet you have to humble your self since you are in training, and only Jesus know what is happen to you at that moment. Since you recognize that Jesus would like you to be like a little child, as a result through his son Jesus Christ he can train you to be like him. Jesus humbles himself to the cross accordingly that he could save all his people from their sins. Therefore I distinguish that I was getting a symbol from God. Jesus Christ would like to covenant with a humble heart! Being angry and may perform things that the Lord may not like to see in your heart will drive the Holy Spirit from you. Jesus loves a humble heart, as a result he can manifest his spirit through you, and as a result you can tell others about his wonderful love for you. When you overcome difficult times? Praise the Lord until the end of time, never gets weary of his strength of character. We should always love one another and be humble towards one another; as a result the humble Spirit can speak to your heart. I discern if every one would make an effort to perform accordingly we would have a superior world. Jesus suffers and dies on the cross for each and every one! Once he came on earth and speak to his people they did not believe his words. Therefore they killed him. John 12: 44, 45 Tell's you that! Jesus cried and said he that believeth on me believeth not on me, but on him that sent me. And he that seeth me seeth him that sent me. Occasionally we have to believe in things we have not seen. We speak of Jesus who we have not seen and yet we endeavor to believe in him and love him! When you see a servant of God speaking! We should always make an effort to be carefully attentive to the words from his or her mouth, because Jesus speaks through them, they are his servants. Try to understand what they are saying! If you do not understand, ask some one to help you to understand, and pray always and ask the good Lord to be of assistance to you in the direction of knowing him, as a result you can understand more about him, when some one speak of him. God have his way of speaking to his people through his servants. Humble your self and try to know Jesus! The only way to know Jesus, you have to humble your self like a little child again. He loves to teach children. Disadvantage will come, but you can over come by humbling your self like a little child. Jesus said! Until you can be like a little child you can not enter into the kingdom of God. Micah 6: 8 Said! He hath shewed thee, O men, what is good; and what doth the Lord require of thee, but to do justly, and to love mercy, and to walk humble with God?

CHAPTER 51
SATAN USED OTHERS TO TAKE ALL I HAD! YET JESUS LET ME SEE HEAVEN EVEN CLEARER!

I get nearer to be acquainted with Jesus he is the greatest of all beams, and when it comes to material things, they can always be replace, knowing the Lord and to love him and obey him and do his will is a wonderful thing. At that time when I was working with the Holy Spirit, it was like I was in a different world. If one should learn to love our Lord Jesus Christ, you would love others and would never think of cheating or steeling. Jesus love when we love and care for others. I have experience things that give me a clearer idea of what Jesus have suffered through for us when he was on earth. I recognize he has die on the cross for us, he also suffer the hands of wicked people. However I did not know that I could experience suffering so close like Jesus. I think on familiar terms with when I was growing up I always look at existence as one that could never failed. I love every thing that was beautiful, and would always endeavor to work heard to achieve all that I need. And there come a time when I was helpless and with out any thing, and I do not give up. And I love the Lord even more, and have a great faith that he will raise me up again. I would like every one to make an effort to show ever one love, and never strive to brake down others, however to assist to fabricate others. As a result that at what time Jesus is using his Holy Spirit to assist someone to be acquainted with the Lord we will recognize that we need to execute being of assistance to them. Jesus is love, peace longsuffering. And he desires us to love one another and have a humble heart; as a result he can also work through you to assist others. I am praying that through the Holy Spirit others will come to be acquainted with the Lord, presently the same as I accomplish. Jesus desires us to discern him and he will permit different things to happen in the direction for you that is true and honest in the sight of God. What he has suffered through, his father could have stopped it from happening to him, however he did not execute for the reason that he desired him to accomplish his work for his purpose of saving his creatures, and the intention of was to saving our souls through the cross. For anyone to have that kind of strength and faith to endure all things, and over come, you have to pray constantly and solicit the good Lord to be of assistance to you in the direction of loving one another. Also in the direction of be acquainted with him you ought to read the Holy Bible with prayer and fasting, and believing that Jesus can assist you to accomplish accordingly. Luke 17: 24, 25 Tell's you that! For as the lighting that lighteneth out of the one part under heaven shineth under the other part under heaven so shall the son of man be in his days. But first must he suffer many things and be rejected of this generation. Therefore since Jesus say we should follow his foot step and endure all things, to discern him, sometimes we have to suffer some of what he has suffered through on earth. He said his determination is that he will not give us more than what we can bear, therefore I recognize that he will put on end to all my suffering, as I put my trust in Jesus, and ask him to help me to over come through prayer and fasting. Jesus cares for us each and every one, let us serve Jesus.

CHAPTER 52

LOOKING TO JESUS AT ALL TIMES, EVEN BEFORE DISAPPOINTMENT COMES!

J esus is a long-suffering son of God! He will give you time for you to be acquainted with him and perform his strength of character. Jesus has a verdict to pass on us, and we should endeavor to make on effort and perform his strength of character before it's too late. When you come to be acquainted with the Lord? It will be uncomplicated to follow his words. Jesus said! He first loved us accordingly we can love him as well. If we love Jesus! It will be uncomplicated to serve him. Looking to Jesus at all times even before disappointment comes, it's very important, as a result when disappointments come, you will be competent to overcome suffering. When I was gaining knowledge to be acquainted with Jesus Christ, through the power of the Holy Spirit, I was in the direction of being like a child. It was like going back to school. It was a step- by - step training. It was freighting because I did not know for sure what was happening to me. I even got sick, because I have to work each day and I was going through different changes, and I have to distinguish Jesus different from Satan to overcome. When the Holy Spirit comes upon you, you have to discern that it's the Holy Spirit of God through his son Jesus Christ. The Holy Spirit will guide you into all truth and righteousness'. After coming to be acquainted with him it was a wonderful experience. You do not want to loose that wonderful feeling in your heart. You will experience difficulty when you are learning, however the only way to overcome is to have strong believed in Christ, and follow him carefully through his words. First you must love him, and desires to serve him. He wants you to love him and put your trust in him always. Even when you come to know the Lord, you will experience difficult times, the world we are living in today with different kind of people to deal with, is not an easy one. You should never give up, trust in the Lord and lean on his understanding constantly, and he will be of assistance to you in the direction toward overcoming all problems. People will always test your faith to see if you will give up and come and execute the things they do or say. When you accept the Lord as your personal savior from sin, even in the church you will experience difficult times, because they are not all perfect. Facilitate those who you can assist and pray constantly, and ask the Lord to be of assistance toward keeping his words, and be faithful to him always. Also ask Jesus to give you the strength toward being of assistance to others. John 17: 1-3 Tell's you that! Jesus speaks these words, to his father! And lifted up his eyes to heaven and said, Father the hour is come Glorify thy son, that thy son also may glorify thee. As thou hast given him power over all flesh that he should give eternal life to as many as thou hast given him. And this is life eternal, that they might know thee thy only true God and Jesus Christ, whom thou hast sent. Jesus turn to his father for assistance, that he may recognize the true and living God. Just keep praying for them and always make an effort to assist others. Once you know the Lord and be of assistance to others, when the Lord comes he will not tell you depart from him, because I know you not. God knows his people, and he knows all who serve him in Spirit and in truth. To know the Lord is very important. When you come to know the Lord our savior Jesus Christ, it will bring joyfulness to your heart. I can remember when I was younger and working for my self, I never think of a gift from any one I always just want to go and buy all that I need! After struggling through difficult times I come to realized that Jesus can give you gift that makes your heart joyful. The gift of knowing God is a gift for life, if you honor Jesus and praise him for the knowledge he has given unto you. He can make all things possible when it seems impossible. Only trust in him always, and pray constantly for understanding and wisdom. God will let you know all that you need to know through his Holy Spirit. The Holy Ghost power will move in a merciful way, and n such a way that you will not even think of earthly things. Jesus is alive, have faith in him and love him before difficult come your way and he will make a way for each and ever one of us.

CHAPTER 53

JESUS SAVE, NO MATTER HOW HOPELESS IT MAY SEEMS! HE CAN SAVE YOU.

On behalf of you to have that believe in you; to know that Jesus can save you from any problems, you have to put your trust in him, and believe in him as you ask for any thing through prayer. Jesus is our strong helper in time of need and always. If we trust in his words, and learn to believe in him, we will be able to get assistance. Praying always and ask him to give you strength to believe in his wards as you read them; he will here and answer prayer. You can read Jesus words and it does not reach your heart or mind, because you do not understand what you read. Understanding comes through Jesus! The only way you can have that strength and understanding, is to believe in him, love him and you must be willing to learn of him. Asking Jesus with a sincere heart to be of assistance toward believing in him, and love him always! Jesus loved each and every one, no matter how hopeless it may seems, he will help you as you come to him with an open heart. He desires you to let him in! As a result he can work in your heart to assist you to believe in him and love him. With out Jesus helping you it will seem hopeless. When you receive his assistance, you should constantly give him thanks for helping you. The best way to give him thanks is to accept him in your life as your savior and Lord. You should always endeavor to be honest and true to his words and his will be there for you! Be ye honest and true! You can also show him honesty by being honest and true to others. Helping others to know the Lord and following his words, your life will be a different one in the sight of the Lord. He will care for you always! And be of assistance to you more. Jesus cares for each and every one and desires us to serve him always. 1 John 1: 9 Tell's you that! If we confess our sins, he is faithful and just to forgive us our sins, and cleanse us from all unrighteousness. When he forgive you all unrighteousness? You should endeavor to avoid all sin. There will be trial and temptation comes your way at all times, you should make an effort not to fall in sin yet again. Go to God in prayer and ask him to assist you in the direction of avoiding sin again, you can not accomplish it on your own!

Only through Jesus you will be able to achieve doing so. Believe that he can be of assistance to you, trust in him and pray always, and make an effort to avoid the things that cause you to sin. Jesus is for eternity there for you! But you can not be on familiar terms with that the things you are doing is sin and keep on doing them, and continue going to the Lord! You will collapse into destruction. As soon as he be of assistance to you in the direction of overcoming sin you will know, Jesus will relief your mind and taught and heart from all pressure. When you be converted into a child of God? You will observe others elsewhere in the world of sin frustrating you, toward acquiring you to come and sin again; you should constantly endeavor and be strong through the terminology of God! And pray to Jesus always. When you are in the house of God you should be extremely careful of the things you declare or execute. Jesus eyes are watching you! You are in his Holy place. Jesus watches you any where you are, however when you accept his words, and say yes to him through baptism, you have to be very careful. Jesus said in! Luke 10: 20 not with standing in this rejoice not, that the Spirit are subject unto you; but rather rejoice, because your names are written in heaven. Jesus cares no matter how hopeless life may seem, trust, have faith and obey him always.

CHAPTER 54

THE GOOD SAMARITAM COMES TO MY HELP!

esus is the Good Samaritan! He is for eternity in close proximity to you when you need him, or yet send you a messenger. As soon as you lay all your dependence on Jesus our savior, you can always depend on him, as you call on him he will answer. I have experience times when I am in difficult moment and God send me a messenger, out of now were to be of assistance to me. I praise him more each day when he opens those doors for me. He is a loving savior! He is always there for me when I needed him. He gives me a free choice to call on him! To call on him, you have to be acquainted with him, to discern him you have to pray to Jesus always to assist you through his Holy Angels. And there is another important step you need to use to be acquainted with him, is to read his Holy Bible continually daily. Jesus needs you to discern him as a result you can constantly call on him when you need him. In health or in suffering! Jesus is there for you always. I have proven him in many different ways. And I know you can prove himself as well. Presently present him in your life and give him a chance of your life and accept him as you Lord and savior Jesus Christ. He loves you and be concerned for you. I could remember when I was going through difficult times and could not speak! My burden was consequently heavy; the words could not come out of my mouth. However I recognize they were in my heart, therefore I take a pen and paper and wrote my prayer to the Lord and things changes for me. When I was able to pray through my mouth, I start praying to the Lord always. I prayed in my bed at night, I prayed in my car. I have even stopped one time and answer to the Holy Angels, as they come upon on me while I was driving. They were accordingly strong in my mind, I could not concentrate on driving, and the Angels at the same time, therefore I know the Lord can help me through his Holy Angels, because I prove him that's why I can enlighten my readers to gaining knowledge of of Jesus through prayer and reading his Holy words. Jesus can come to you in different form; he can even use the people around you to test your faith towards him. He can place his Angels in their hearts and tell them what to accomplish form you, as a result you may discern him. It's best for ever one to be acquainted with Jesus, therefore that when he knocks at your heart door, you will open and give permission in. As you let him in he will reveal himself to you and you will love him and desires to serve him until he comes. St John 17: 1- 26 Tell's you that! Jesus has spoken words, and lifts up his eyes to heaven and said! Father the hour is come Glorify thy son, that thy son also may glorify thee. He said! O father the world hath not knower thee but I have known thee and these have known that thou hast sent me. When the "messenger" has come unto you and you are on familiar terms with the Lord, you will be able to use these words in this scripture. The words are great and marvelous and sure word, because Jesus has known his father he depend on him always. Therefore if you should come to be acquainted with Jesus through praying and fasting and reading his words you will be able to advise others that Jesus love them as well. Jesus cares for each and every one trust in his words.

CHAPTER 55

THE HEALING POWER OF GOD, I HAVE EXPERIENCE! GOD GREAT AND MARVELOUS WORK THROUGH WORKING IN THE NURCING CARE!

My patient I was taking care of in the month of May, and June of 1999, was in a terrible condition. When I went to the home where he live and see him, his feet were in a very bad condition, I did not say a word, and I look after him and watch him heal and was able to walk again. On the last day I work for him, he said to me, I cannot get over how my feet have been healed. The Doctor was planning to surgically remove my feet! And now I am getting better and able to walk. That's when I say to him that's the power of God! He is the one who heal you. You should never give up on him at any time, as he is able to perform all things. When the Doctor give up? God never give up. Those are words of comfort I leave with him. Jesus always brings joy to my heart when I see his wonderful work. I am aware that I can not accomplish any thing on my own; however through the Holy power of God nothing is impossible. You merely have to believe in him and trust in him. When you come to know the good Lord and savior Jesus Christ, you will be able to lay all your trust in him, knowing that he can accomplish all things for you and through you. Your bodies is the temple of God, and as you use it in the right order, God will able to used his Holy Spirit within you to be of assistance to others and you. 11 Corinthians 6:16 said! And what agreement hath the temple of God with Idol? For ye are the temple of the living God; as God hath said, I will dwell in them, and walk in them; and I will be their God, and they shall be my people. So I am advising you to pray always, read God Holy words and try to do the things that are right in his sight, and you will come to be acquainted with Jesus as your savior and Lord. Jesus is the healing baming Gillard! Serve him.

CHAPTER 56

JESUS IS THE GREATEST HELPER OF ALL! HE LOVES YOU, AND WANT'S YOU TO PUT YOUR TRUST IN HIM!

Jesus said! I f you put your trust in him he will make your way straight! St. John 6: 47, 48 Tell's you that verily, verily, I say unto you. He that believeth on me hath everlasting life. I am the bread of life. Jesus is your source of life, and your strength, when you can depend on him. He loves you and desires you to trust in him, and follow his wards carefully. He guides you when you are down and when you are up. Let him leads you into righteousness'. Open your hearts to him he wants to come in. He is always knocking at your heart door, he is always sending messengers to your heart door, it could be through a book or someone come to your door, or even on the street, Just stop for a moment and listen to the good wards from above. He cares, and he desires you to care as well. Jesus said! You should seek him and he will answer to all your needs. You have to know him, believe in him as a result he can work within your heart and be of assistance to you. Loving Jesus as your personal savior from sin is the first step to knowing him. As soon as you love Jesus he will help you to understand his words. He is a true savior, he his pleading for you, because he desires you to be saving in his kingdom. He first walks the rugged road for each and every one. He gave his life for us on the cruel cross. He suffers and dies, and was raised on the third day, just to let us recognize that he love us. His father could stop all the wicked men from killing him. He has no sin but yet he die for us. The reason for dying on the cross is for each and every human bean to be saved in his kingdom. Jesus desires us in the direction of being able to be saved in his father's kingdom. After he was raised on the third day, he went to his father before he could perform the will of his father. God is peppering for us he said he his gone to prepare a place for us that where he is there we may be also. St. John 14:1-3 Said! Let not your heart be troubled: ye believe in God believe also in me. In my father's house are many mansions: if it were not so, I would tell you. I go to prepare a place for you. And if I go and prepare a place for you, I will come again and receive you unto my self; that where I am, there ye may be also. Jesus is our life! He cares for us, and desired us to save us in his father kingdom. He also desires us to have a free choice. Therefore all he asks us to accomplish is to follow his foot step. Jesus said the word is life and the word is he. John 6: 63 Said! It is the spirit that quickeneth; the flesh profiteth nothing; the words that I speak unto you, they are spirit, and they are life. If you read his words and perform them as he ask you to do! You will be able to go into his father's kingdom. Jesus is the greatest father of all, he is our advocate, love him and trust in him, and constantly worship him.

CHAPTER 57

TO KNOW JESUS YOU HAVE TO LOVE HIM! TO KNOW YOURSELF YOU HAVE TO BE TAUGHT FROM A CHILD

When I was a child, I have on experience about the Lord, when I become a woman; I have the same experience as when I was a child. While I was going to school; I got my first child at the age of 15 years of age. After having my baby I got married at the age of 17 years of age. I have to stay home and take care of my child; I could not go back to school at that moment. I had a second child 2 years later, and after having my third child. I decided I want to go back to school again. I start going to a commercial school and start learning shorthand and typing, of which I did well. I love secretarial job, therefore I wanted was to achieve the certificate, as a result I could work. I had to stop again, because I got pregnant with my forth child again, after having the baby I start going back to school. I went to Dint hill T. high school to finish my course. I did the entire course and went to take the exam, I failed it I was very surprised when I did not pass, because I was a. student with A & B Report. I had a dream when I was about 17 years of age, I saw tree men in the cloud and the one in the middle had a crown on his head, and the Ten Commandments written in big bold letters beside them. I recognize that the Lord was speaking to me through that dream. I start traveling to be of assistance to my husband in supporting my children. I go to different country to buy clothing and shoes and housing items and take back to Jamaica and sell them to other people. After I went to London to visit my family I had another dream, the dream was speaking to me again. I was told in the dream what to drink for my tummy. And I was told that I would be speaking in a church with many people. I went back to Jamaica, I got the things I dream and used it as I was told. I leave to the U.S.A. I start having difficult times, and during that time I start learning as if I was going to school. The training takes place while I was at work, on the road in my car. I went to school for a short time in the U.S.A. I was still doing English and typing. I was told one day while I was in my car that I was going to have a little girl baby, and she was going to be white. At the moment I did not have a husband or seeing any one. Shortly after I start seeing some one I wanted was to get married again because my first marriage was broken. I was in a lonely state at that time therefore I was impressed to have a relationship through my friend that encourages me to do so. I got pregnant and have a little girl. Then the schooling from heaven began to get stronger. I had to stay home with the baby despite the fact that I could not go to work. I lost my car and other things that I own. I was having on experience; I did not want to stop. God was schooling me I have gone through so much difficult times Nevertheless,

I overcome. I come to recognize what was happening then, therefore I worry no more. Psalm119: 98, 99, Said! Thou through thy commandments hast made me wiser than mine enemies: for they are ever with me. I have more understanding than my teacher: for thy testimonies are my meditations. To be acquainted with Jesus sometimes you have to suffer, to discern more about your self, you have to go to school. Jesus loves each and ever one, trust in his words. Jesus is the only one who can help us to help our children! Therefore we have to depend on him always. A child has to be Constance in training to be able to keep the love of God in their hearts. Therefore we as parents and teachers as we have them in our care, we should take great responsibility in seeing that they are learning all that they are taught. And we as parents should always pray to the Lord for guiding angels, to lead and direct bough parents and children. Jesus is the answer to all our problems! He wishes us to depend on him for our needs. We should always try to give our hearts to Jesus; as a result the life we live can also help our children to follow us. When a child has to come in this world, and has to face a life of despair, because of those same human beans or others. It's very difficult for that child to live with those problems, and to be trained in school. A child is Jesus angel! That child has to be trained by those parents or others. I can bear the pain of adult going through a period of suffering; however I cannot stand the sight of seeing or hearing of a child suffering. A child is not responsible for no problem on adult may be going through. Adult are responsible to care and trained that child. I have been going through pain and suffering for over 20 years. A child came into the picture, I think that child should get happiness and not suffering, that child is on angel send from God. We should care for her and see that the child dose not have suffering in this world. She has been facing difficult times with me alone. I can tell you it gives me great pain to see what she is going through with me. Nevertheless God is always in the picture, he gives me faith and courage to go on each day. She always has a smile on her face. She chairs me up by telling me mammy when I look at you I see expectation. That comes from her mouth! It comes straight from a mouth of on angel. God keep and care for her, therefore it gives me anticipation as she speaks. I always said never give up, trust in the Lord and he will always take care of you. Therefore I know the Lord speak through me as well. I was taught from on early age from my mother to have faith in God. Therefore I always do so. No matter how hopeless it may seem. Jesus cares and knows each and every one. He is always there to help us. We should take every responsibility to see our children formulate to be on adult seeing that we are parents. A child suffering is unbearable! Therefore we should train and take care of them at on early age. Genesis 17: 7 Tell's you that! And the Lord will establish my covenant between me and thee and thy seed after thee in their generation for an everlasting covenant, to be able to train our children as God also used his angel to train us. The child will be able to train his or her children as Jesus did for us. What a wonderful world that would be?

CHAPTER 58

THE HEALING POWER OF GOD IS A GIFT FROM GOD!

God give me a gift, as a result I can be of assistance to others in the direction of them being heal from sickness and even out of problems that we have in our in our daily lives. When he used his servants to be of assistance to others, Jesus would like to recognize that we give him thanks and praise, or even a gift in his sight. When you say thanks to the savior he will continues to give his servants more strength and wisdom, knowledge and understanding to be of assistance to others. God is love! Give thanks and praise to God. It is so wonderful when you can be relief from pain and suffering, and to know that Jesus is the solitary who perform great miracles, as a result the pain could leave your body. Why not give him thanks? We should always glorify his mighty and powerful name. He loves us and care for us all! And he desires us to magnify him. Mark 1: 40-45 Tell's you that! And there come a man full of leper to Jesus beseeching him and kneeling down to him and saying unto him. If thou wilt thou canst make me clean. And Jesus move with compassion, put forth his hand and touched him, and saith unto him, I will be thou clean. And immediately the leprosy departed from him. And he was cleansed. And he strictly charges him, and forth with send him away and saith unto him, see thou say nothing to any man: but go thy way, shew thyself to the priest, and offer for thy cleansing those things which Moses commanded for a testimony unto them. He went out and began to publish it much and to blaze aboard the matter. Insomuch that Jesus could no more openly enter into the city, but was with out in desert places: and they came to him from every quarter. Therefore you can see from this scripture that the man gives thanks to Jesus by telling others that he has been healed by Jesus, which is the son of God. It brings joy to Jesus and he began to help all that comes to see him through the man that received healing. That was his way of giving thanks. Always remember to give thanks to Jesus for his healing power, or even his servants. God can also help you through your doctor. Once you are better and heal give him thanks in what ever way God lead your heart to show thanks. He here and answer prayer. Jesus knows us by name and nature; he knows what he does for us and what he doesn't do. If we able to show thanks to Jesus he will know you by name and nature, and continue to bless you. Telling others are also giving thanks, giving a gift in his name is also saying thanks. Praising him and serving him for the rest of your life is also giving thanks, that's even greater thanks to God. Jesus rejoices over one sinner that repents. Repentance can come through help! When he helps you praise him always! Jesus is the great healer; however he can use his servants to heal his people as well. Therefore we need to be acquainted with Jesus work that when the Holy Spirit comes upon his servants and give command to heal the sick ones you will discern that is the Lord who gives authority to help you through his healing Angels. Jesus is the strength of all; just give him thanks as you recognize him. He loves you and always cares for each and every one. To be acquainted with the Lord and his healing command was not easy; nevertheless I come to realized that I have to follow his foot step to discern him. I could see that I was carrying the symbol of the cross as a partaker of Jesus Christ suffering. Heavenly training is like I was in space some times. Therefore put your trust in God, and have a humble heart, as a result he can reveal himself to you. Amen.

CHAPTER 59
GOD HOLY SERVANTS IS EVERY WERE!

We as teachers, and parents should take careful attention to our children as they grew. God may need to use one as his humble servant. And because we may neglect that child, because he or she do not have high stander or education, or may not look beautiful as we want them to be, that child may have to suffer to be acquainted with God, and they are all God beautiful children in their own way! We should love them all as God love us all. We should find that child who was neglected through God heavenly power. He knows our hearts and mind; he knows who he wants for heavenly training. We should teach all children with one love, in the sight of God. Love leads and direct always! First we should pray constantly, to the Lord and ask him to assist us in the up growing of our children. When we trained them at on early age, God will help them to know him at on early age. Sometimes God will even stop that child or person along the way, just to give them heavenly training. It can be difficult times, because God used Holy Spirit to train him or her to accomplish his work. Jesus is the greatest of all trainers! He can train in different ways. He loves you! If he want you to perform his will, he will leads you in ever way that seem best to him. Therefore you can be acquainted with him and recognize what he desires you to accomplish? Matthew 12: 50 Tell's you that! For whosoever shall do the will of my father, which is in heaven, the same is my brother and sister, and mother. Therefore in teaching our children to accomplish the will of God we become brothers, and sisters and mothers and fathers for them as we become like Jesus. Jesus cares for each and every one! Follow his words as you read and as you lead by his servants, they are ever were Jesus is leading them to find you and tell you about his love for you.

CHAPTER 60
OVER COMING POWER IS REAL!

In the year of 1977 one night I was home with my children, and I heard a knocking at my house door, I went and answer the door. As soon as I open the door I saw one of my husband co-worker at the door, I know my husband was at work, so I panic for a moment, I was told by him that that my husband was in on accident at the plant where he was working, and a lot of men wore burn to death and some was in the hospital. I was so shock I started to cry, and he told me he was going to take me down to the hospital. I got dress and went with him to the hospital. It was unbearable to see what had happen to the men. My mother and Dad had just come from London, therefore I ask my mom to sit with the children as a result I could go to the hospital each day. We had them move to another hospital which was one of the best in the Jamaica. I help to take best care of him until he was able to be back at home. In the year of 1980 my father went back to London, because my mother went to London, and he was sick and he taught going back to London, he would have better doctors to be of assistance to him. After he went back early in 1980, he started to get more sick, therefore he wrote to me and told me he was sick however he would soon be better, about one week later my brother received a telegram telling him that my father was dead. He came to my house and told me, I did not believe because I just heard from him and he said he would be better. I could not stop crying, the pain was unbearable. My mother wrote me and told me she and my family were going to assist me to come to London, but they could not assist me to come to the funeral. Therefore later in the year they send me a ticket to come and visit them for 3 months. I got the visa and went to London for 3 months. While I was there I got a vision, telling me what I should drink to help my tummy and that I was going to be preaching in a church. It was a very well spend time, after the visit was over I went back to Jamaica to my family, I spend a short time with my children and husband, and I leave to U.S.A. on the 15ᵗʰ of December 1980. I wanted was to come to the U.S.A. to work and be of assistance to my family because my husband was no longer working. I arrived at New York airport, one of my friends came to get me at the airport, and I stay at my friend home for three weeks. I was told that my brother and wife were in Florida, therefore I called him and he invited me to come to Florida because the climate was nice, and was like Jamaica. I leave New York and came to Florida, I start working and help my self and my family in Jamaica. During the time I was with him I was working hard, my life began to change, I would be at work and I was working in space. I started hearing the Holy Spirit speaking to me. Sometimes I would stop my car and be at peace and answer to the Holy Spirit. I used to worry and cry I even had to go to the hospital for a nervous brake down. I have a friend and she told me I should go with her and see a spiritual lady who she know, when I go there she told me I should pray and burn white candles and use olive oil to rub my body. I leave the lady and told my friend God can be of assistance to me, I start to realize that it was God Holy Spirit was trying to get me to perform his will. The moment I come to discern Jesus my tears was dry up, and I just turn to Jesus. My children were all in Jamaica I could not go back at the moment. Therefore I keep in touch with then through writing and telephone calls. I send things for them and money, until I start having problems and could not manage to do so any more. During my difficult times I was driving home from work and the Holy Spirit told me I was going to have a white baby girl. I did not have a husband or a friend at the moment. I happen to be at home on a Sunday and my room mate told me there was a festival T.Y. Park in Hollywood, I should go with her, I drove down there with her, and there I met my daughter father. I was divorcé and alone, therefore we start having a relationship. We talk about getting married however I would not do so, because I did not think it was right at the moment, there was a problem that needs to be taken care of. He insists seeing me, and my daughter comes along. I even told my baby father I could not have a relationship with out being married. After having the baby, I start learning more about the Lord. Therefore I say to my self this must be one of God necessary doing. I rush the baby to church and got her blessed. I ask the father to go to church with me and get the baby blessed, because I could see that God was using the baby with me to discern more about him. I start to suffer more because I lost my job, lost my car, and the father said he lost his car and was unable to be of assistance to me and the baby any more. I had an operation to have my baby and was unable to go back to work early. God was on my side helping me in many ways, until I was able to go to work again. I go to several different jobs and was unable to keep any because of the baby. God has brought me through and give me faith to overcome. I turn to Jesus on the 15th of December1991, I was with the Lord from I was 12 years old, but after coming to recognize him I renewed my vows on the 15th of December 1991. When I fully see what he required me to accomplish, I accept his calling and on my way to glory. I prayed for all of my children and ask the good Lord to take care of them because I was unable to take care of them, with his assistance he answer me in plain words and tell me he will take care of them. I went to see them in 1993 and they were well taken care of. My baby daughter got baptize at the age of 7 years old. And all the rest is baptize and one is a poster of the Seventh-Day-Adventist church. He was trained at the West Indies collage. So I promise the good Lord that I will perform his will until he comes. He has given me over coming power as a result I could overcome any obstacle in my life, he is a wonderful savior! He cares for each and every one. Trust and obey him always.

CHAPTER 61
TO KNOW THE LORD BEFORE SAYING YES TO HIM IS VERY IMPORTANT!

J esus is true, honest, loving, and sure savior. When you come to be acquainted with him, you will never desire to leave him. Make an effort to discern Jesus through reading his words and praying for understanding. The word is Jesus! Once you come to know Jesus you will never want's to leave his presents. At what time trials and temptation come your way, you should constantly depend on Jesus and put him first in your live, he is sure and caring! Give Jesus a chance in your life; let him help you in all things. Some times it will be like life is hopeless, immediately get on your knees and pray, even if you are in your car pray, or at work call on Jesus any were you are. He here and answer prayer. You may need to go shopping; the first thing you need to distinguish is what you are going shopping for! As you know what you are shopping for, it becomes easer to go. The same way it will be as you come to be acquainted with the Lord, you will always say I will desire him in my life and never wish for him to leave my presents. Always try to recognize what you desire, or what you are getting into before you get into it. Jesus desires you to be acquainted with him, consequently that are the reason why he gives us a choice. He request of you to chouse freely, he could let ever one chose him with out giving us a chance to chouse; however he did not do so for the reason that he desires us to have freedom of choice, and know right from wrong. Jesus is Lord and savior of all. 1 John 2: 4, 5 Tell's you that! He that saith, I know him and keepeth not his commandments is a liar, and the truth is not in him. But whoso keepeth his word in him verily is the love of God perfected: hereby know we that we are in him. Therefore from these words from the Bible you can see that when you come to be acquainted with what you are getting into, your heart will be at peace to accomplish the will of God. I have come to recognize the Lord in such a way that I give my life to him, and trying to accomplish his will. I even see the pain of others and devote my self to helping them, in such a way that I almost give up on earthly things. There is time when I can only see the beautiful light of heaven, in such a way that I feel rich inside of me. I just feel that I have it all. I could see some times like no one care about me on earth any more, nevertheless I recognize someone cares for the reason that he proves him self to me and I discern he is with me. Sometimes I feel that I am at the end of the rope, and right there and then Jesus step in and show me the way. And he let me know I must not give up. Jesus cares! I have a dream in October of 2000! I went to bed about 1am I have seen two people came to me and told me that they are going to give me all that I need. I recognize right there and then that the good Lord is working in my life to give me a special life. It brings joy to my heart, for the reason that I recognize he have his angels watching over me. And he is telling me some way that he will take care of me. Jesus is the answer I am just waiting on Jesus to give me the right progress. I come to the U.S.A. and I work 16 hours per day to take care of my children and my self. And all that I bought for my self was taking from me. Therefore I came to a stop where I just have to move according to his riches in glory, and then he will allow me keep what he has in store for me. Jesus is the answer to all our problems; he always cares for each and every one. Immediately allow him in your hearts and see his marvelous work. Jesus is waiting patiently for us to answer his calling. Proverbs 3: 5, 6 Tell's you that! You should trust in the Lord with all thine heart, and lean not unto thine own understanding. In all thy ways acknowledge him, and he shall direct thy parts. Jesus cares for each and ever one, as you come to discern him, trust in his words, and by no means leave him. Jesus is love!

CHAPTER 62

JESUS IS TRUE, HONEST, LOVING, AND SURE SAVIOR, WHEN YOU COME TO KNOW HIM, YOU WILL NEVER WANT'S TO LEAVE HIM!

Jesus is love! Love is true, honest, loving and sure. You ought to believe in Jesus words to be able to have this beautiful mind of Jesus. To be true, is pure! You should endeavor to be true in all that you execute or articulate. Honest is very important in the sight of God! God is sure and honest to us in is promises; he loves us once we are honest to each others. Loving also is also very important it gives us a pure heart, for the reason that Jesus is love! If we love each others on earth we will be able to love the father son and the Holy Spirit. Love is the fulfillment of God Commandments. To be sure about what you say or do is very important. At what time you say yes to Jesus through baptism, you should be sure about what you are getting into. When you are sure, you will be able to keep those vows. They are God Holy words and they should be kept. To discern Jesus his father and Holy Ghost, you have to have all those qualities. Those qualities are Jesus! As you distinguish them you will by no means desires to leave his presences? He will let you love him with on everlasting love that never changes. Jesus love his people, he is pleading to each and every one to accept his wonderful love that he has given to us, it's just for us to seek him through his words and follow them. Jesus suffers and dies on the cross for each and every one, because he loves us with on everlasting love! It's uncondisitional. Trust in his words his promises are sure he never failed, I have suffered to know Jesus! But it was for all the good reasons. I love him back because he first love me, in favor of Jesus in the direction of proving to me that he loved me he have to permit things to leave me, however I am happy he could allow me to know him. As soon as you know him you will observe why he had to allow these things happen to you. God gave his only son to die on the cross, in the direction of saving us in his father's kingdom! That love is unbearable to any one who has a child and knows what it like to have your child, and have to give him up to die. He is our father, what more can he do to prove to us that he loves us and want us to be save in his father kingdom. I think that is the greatest love of all. Jesus does as his father ask him to do! That is love. There is no other love greater than that love. Trust in his words and follow them, he desires to save us all. Job 13: 15 Tell's you that! Though he slay me, yet will I trust in him; but I will maintain mine own ways before him. Solomon's Song 8: 6 Tell's you that! Set me as a seal upon thine heart, as a seal upon thine arms: for love is strong as death; jealousy is cruel as the grave: The coals there of are coals of fire, which hath a most vehement flame. St. Luke 8: 15 Tell's you that! But that on the good ground are they, which is on Honest and good heart, having heard the word, keep it and bring forth fruit with patience. Acts 6: 3 Said! Wherefore, brethren, look ye out among you seven men of honest report. Full of the Holy Ghost and Wisdom whom we may appoint over this business. Therefore as you read these scriptures you will observe how God treat people with love and honesty. Let us put our heart with Jesus and he will assist you to have all those qualities. With out those qualities we will not be able to manage in this sinful world and over come and enter into our father's kingdom. Follow Jesus words, and trust in them, they are life and true, and pure.

CHAPTER 63

TO LEARN IS VERY IMPORTANT IN THE SIGHT OF GOD AND MAN! IN GOD'S EYE YOU HAVE TO LEARN OF HIM. IN THE EYES OF MAN YOU HAVE TO LEARN THE EARTLY THINGS OF LIFE

With out knowledge no one would be acquainted with right from wrong. I could remember the days when I did not learn the way in witch God desires me to go! It was a very terrifying experience for me. To gain knowledge of God was a very difficult one, because the mischievous sprite was like a rearing lion trying to stop the Holy Spirit from training his servant. Nevertheless Jesus has proved to his servant that he is God and is able to let Satan recognize that he rules. Therefore he gives me the strength to overcome all fears. The earthly learning is a difficult experience as well, the different is you can give up on earthly training, but you can not give up on God training. The earthly training is also important for us to be acquainted with, because it helps us to deal with the things of this earth. We should take time out as we can to learn earthly training it can help us to be stronger in God's training. Loving the Lord Jesus is very important obsession to accomplish; to love Jesus is to know him! When you come to discern Jesus it's a beautiful feeling, you will always have joy in your hearts. Love gives you the opportunity to say yes to Jesus through baptism. There is one other beautiful love Jesus can give you, the feeling of affection to show some one, which you can say yes, in the direction of marriage. There is a special gift from God which is marriage and baptism! They are special vows from God; we should utilize them with special respect. If you recognize the true and living God whom we serve, you will respect those two vows. We should take careful taught towards them before we used them. The reason why we should take special care is because God is a very important God, and we should respect and love him always. If we all learn in the direction of achieving knowledge of those vows, we will have less turning back out of the Churches, and we will have less divorces. When we divorce we are breaking the special gift from God? When we do not be acquainted with the true love from God, and we used it wrong and then we end up in divorce court, we can get forgiveness, because we did not recognize Jesus love. Knowing the true love from God is very, very important. We can save broken hearts, broken homes, and broken marriages and we will not break the promise we made to God through baptism. God does not desire us to have a broken home or broken marriages, which cause hearts ekes and pain, for parents and children or evens others to endure difficulties they have to acknowledge God, through reading his words and prayer. A marriages that is not through true love from God, is a sin and should not be done. That is why so many children suffer and parents killing one another's. For people to use the Holy mattew money they should be in true love. God is love! And for us to tell others about God's love we should learn to love with ours hearts. Jesus words are true love, we should respect them! The words we speak should come from God. Loving Jesus and respecting him and putting him first in your hearts is very important, as a result we can ask him to guide us in all that we perform or say. Jesus cares and loves us all! And he desires us to gain knowledge of him! Learning is very important.

CHAPTER 64
WHEN YOU BECOME INSPIRED IN THE LORD AND SAVIOR JESUS CHRIST!

To be inspired, you have to be able to understand! Understanding comes from God. To know God you have to love him, and be able to follow his words. Inspirations come from the word of God, and through his Holy Spirit. When you know all those qualities about God's words, you can be inspired. The word is God! As you are acquainted with God and are able to follow his words you will be inspired through his Holy Spirit. You will experience one of the most beautiful feelings you could ever feel. The heart will be joyful and you will be glorious and praising God. To feel Jesus in your heart is wonderful! Jesus is love. And if you allow Jesus in your heart you will be talented to be inspired. Jesus gift is a special gift! We should all try to understand who Jesus is and what he stands and intended for. Acts 8: 18-21 Tell's you that! When Simon saw that through lying on of the apostles' hands the Holy Ghost was given, he offered them money. Saying, give me also this power that on whomsoever I lay hands; he may receive the Holy Ghost. But Peter said unto him, the money perish with thee, because thou hast thought that the gift of God may purchased with money, thou hast nighter part nor lot in his matter, for thy heart is not right in the sight of God. Therefore you can see from this scripture that the gift of God is not a mere curiosity It dose not come easily, it come's from the true and living God. We should always love the Lord with our hearts as a result we can know the gift that comes from him. Jesus is real; you should make an effort to discern him through his words.

CHAPTER 65

THE CHOUSEN ONE, WHICH SENT FROM GOD! OUR FATHER IN HEAVEN!

A t what time a person is chosen through God Son Jesus Christ to be a servant of God? We ought to have great esteem for that person, for the reason that the person that work with you do not work of himself or herself. They work through the Jesus, who speaks through them. Jesus knows each and every one, and he is the solitary who makes all diction for the missioner. We do not have the authority to depilate God missioner work. God come in the form of a man and ask Peter to baptize him, as a result he could perform the work for his father, and that we his children could follow him. Jesus said follow me and I will make you fisher of men. We should endeavor to be like Jesus, not change his rules or make Laws that is not accepted in the sight of God. Matthew 5: 48 Tell's you that! Be ye therefore perfect even as your father which is in heaven is perfect. Also Isaiah 49: 1-3 Tell's you that! Listen, O, isles unto me; and hearken, ye people from far; the Lord hath called me from the womb; from the bowels of my mother hath he made mention of my name. And he hath made my mouth like a sharp sword; in the shadow of his hand hath he hid me, and made me a polish shaft; in his quiver hath he hid me. And said unto me, "thou art my servant, O Israel, in whom I will be glorified." These words are true words from God Holy book! He is asking us to follow his son, accordingly through him we will be able to enter into his father kingdom. He also said! No one come to the father, with out entering through the son. Jesus desires us in the direction of following his words, not change them. Jesus work has to be done, that why the training is so heard! The school of knowledge is wisdom, understanding, and learning of him through the Holy Spirit. We leave to school in the direction of being educated from what we taught, and we understand it. The school of knowledge is in mind, body and soul; God is the only one who used the body, mind, and soul in the right way, as a result we can understand his will. We should respect God training and not change it in different ways. By showing respect to God words that's how we understand; as a result we can be saving in his kingdom.

If we do not have respect for God words, when we go to school we will not be able to learn the earthly training. Jesus is the way, the truth and the life. We should follow him. God knows us all by name and nature, it will take time for a person to know Jesus and love him. In order for us to follow Jesus, we must be acquainted with him and love him. Once you come to know Jesus, the Holy Spirit will work in your heart, and mind, and you will follow his words, and never change his marvelous work. He his true and living savior! God has his chosen people who he wants to do his will; as a result the way can be prepared for his coming. He searches our hearts and mind and knows who desires him in, Jesus does not force any one to accept his will, and he gives us free a choice. We must be familiar with what we desire in life! Jesus or Satan, once we can make those choices, then he will be able to help us to follow him. We can not accomplish his strength of character on our own. Therefore we must love Jesus in our hearts pray constantly for the guiding of the Holy Spirit to help us. Jesus is a wonderful savior! He will never leave you or forsake you; you just have to let him in your hearts and mind! He is a savior who will always keep his promise. Deuteronomy 28: 1-4 Tell's you that! And it shall come to pass, if you shall hearkens diligently unto the voice of the Lord thy God, to observe and do all his commandments which I command thee, this day, that the Lord thy God will set thee on high above all nation of the earth. And all these blessings shall come on thee, and overtake thee, if thou shalt hearken unto the voice of the Lord thy God. Blessed shalt be the city, and blessed shalt thou be in the field. Blessed shall be the fruit of thy body, and the fruit of thy ground and the fruit of thy cattle, the increase of thy kind and the flocks of thy sheep. These are God's sure words! We should learn them by reading them, and make an effort to keep them, as a result the good Lord can restored blessing on us. God chosen one should know him through his words and his Holy Spirit! Jesus love's us why not serve him as we know him?

CHAPTER 66

GOD WORK NEED TO HAVE HONEST PEOPLE, CARE GIVING PEOPLE, LOVING PEOPLE, AND HEARD WORKING PEOPLE TO SAVE SOULS FOR HIS KINGDOM!

Jesus the son of God, need us all to be honest in ever way, as a result we can used our hearts and minds in his honor and glory. He desires us to be like him. Jesus said! Through his prophets in James 1: 18-21 Tell's you that! Of his own will begat he us with the word of truth, that we should be a kind of first fruits of his creatures. Wherefore, my beloved brethren, let every man be swift to here, slow to speak, slow to wrath. For the wrath of man worketh not the righteousness of God. Wherefore lay apart all filthiness and superfluity of naughtiness and receive with meekness the engrafted word, which is able to save your souls. Jesus is love! If we follow his love designed for us, we will be able to accomplish all things through him, with out his words to guide us; our strength of character we will unable to keep his words. His words are life! His words will help you to be saved in his kingdom. We should be able to read, or here his words, subsequently we are able to be saved in his kingdom. When you are called to be a servant of God! We must be able to be honest, trustworthy, loving, and kind to others, and must be able to tell others about God's love and his wonderful words. God see all we perform are saying, we can not hide from him, when we can hide from our family and friends! We can not hide from God. The Judgments day is coming! When Jesus will say to his people come onto me, or depart from me, I know you not! How heard that would be? When you know you are the one that read his words and trying to save people for his kingdom? And he will say depart from me because you have done evil to your brothers and sisters. How would you feel? We should work to go in God's kingdom. When a child had to suffer because of impurity among us? That's call wickedness. I have a child that I have seen suffer because of wickedness towards her mother, which is God servant. I am hurt more for my daughter than myself, because she is a child, one of God angel.

We should stop fighting for what we want! That's the Holy sprit can used our hearts and not Satan. Satan can use your heart in ways you would not believe. If you love the Lord Jesus Christ with all your heart and let Jesus used you, Satan will not have a part in your heart. Pray ever day, read your Bible ever day as a result the love of God can be in your heart constantly. Jesus is love, peace and joy; we should put him first in our hearts. Do not give permission to Satan, allow Jesus in, he will not have any chance to be able to come in your heart. Your heart can be the wickedest part of a human body. Therefore keep it clean by putting Jesus in it. When we hate, fight for things we can not get or what is not ours or even lies, we are putting Satan in our hearts, and there is where Satan began to use your heart, to do wickedness. With out Jesus you will be doom. Give permission to Jesus, to come in your heart! He loves each and every one, and wants us to be saving in his father kingdom. Why not love Jesus back! Jesus work is very important! The importance of his work, he needs truth, honest, and heard working people. Purity is Jesus; serve him he cares for each and every one.

CHAPTER 67

WORKING FOR A HONEST LIVING! JESUS SAID! WE SHOULD LIVE BY THE SWEET OF OUR BROW

Depending on others when you are able to perform several category of work, is not acceptable in the sight of God! I have experience times when I was unable to work for a week pay or a day pay, how heard it was for me. But there was an especially good reason why I could not work at that time. I am a person who constantly loves to work for my self to make a living. There was times when I was in serious training from the Lord, after I had my baby daughter. I was unable to work at the time and I have extremely difficult times. But the good Lord takes me through with my earnest prayer. He provide for me in many different ways. He provides help for me from the U.S. Government. Of which I was very greatful for. I was depending on the Government for a very long time, they help me with schooling, money for my rent and others things. I prayed that God will for ever bless the United State of America! Jesus provided a job for me, as a result I could used to pay my bills and help my daughter Kimberly. I have other children in Jamaica which I have not seen for many years, I could not even help them at that time as I used to execute. I am praying that the good Lord will keep me working, so I will be able to go and see them and do what I would like to accomplish for them. Before Kimberly come along, I used to work and take care of those children. They are all grown now! Therefore it's not such a great responsibility for me any more. It's a wonderful feeling when you can work an honest salary. Jesus loves a person that can work for them selves. The Bible says, by the sweet of thy brow thou shall live. I would like to assist others to gain knowledge of the working for them, and feel that joyful feeling of independent! What ever a person as to perform while you have health and strength we should accomplish as a result with joy. Dependence is unhealthy for all human beans! It's disadvantage regarding depending on others! Jesus is the merciful and loving Savior, he never failed you can depend on him at all time. To be able to have the kind of dependence, you must be save, by accepting Jesus Christ in your heart, and mind and believe that when you ask him for any thing in prayer he will grant it unto you. To depend on God is to have faith in Jesus, through his love for us. We must be able to have faith in God through his son Jesus Christ. At what time you come to know the Lord, you will find that it is a very easy thing to accomplish, Loving Jesus with all your heart, you will find love and strength to endure. Strength to over come and strength to believe that he will provide for you in many different ways, God has his angels and he will send them any were he needs them to go in the direction of seeking help for his servants. Jesus said! By the sweet of your brow we shall live! In the sight of Jesus, we should be honest, heard working in God's eyes. Zechariah 8: 16 Tell's you that! These are the things that you should do! Speak ye every man the truth to neighbor, execute the judgment of truth and peace in your gates. 11 Timothy 3: 17 Tell's you that! The man of God may be perfect, thoroughly furnished unto all good works.

Therefore when we do a good job in the sight of God, he will give us peace and happiness. To know the Lord, you will face with trial and tribulation; you have to know ways and means to over some all trial. Working for an honest living and keeping busy is a very important way of overcoming obstaticle and difficult times, put your trust in the Lord, and pray always. He will here and delivered you!

CHAPTER 68

DISCOVERING THE PLAN OF SALVATION! AND OF TO RETURN BACK TO THE WORLD OF SIN!

The Lord plan of salvation is a sure and perfect one! Where there is not surety and perfection, there is trouble and sinfulness? Therefore if you need help to manage! You have to go for it where it's right. God understand where there is need for necessity, he will forgive you. Jesus care for us all, and would like us to save souls for his kingdom. When I seek for help and received help, I go back to Jesus in sincerity and ask forgiveness for all that I have done, and he grant it unto me. Jesus knows our needs and our pain; he is the great healer and advisor. We should depend on Jesus and he will lead you all the way, he will guide you safely under his wings. The song writer said! Safely through another week God has brought us on our way; Let us now a blessing seek, waiting in his courts today, Day of all the week the best, emblem of eternal rest. While we seek supplies of grace through the dear redeemer name, show thy reconciling face; take away our sin and shame, from our worldly care set free may we rest this day in thee. The song is found in the S.D.A. Hymnal book, the number is 384! After reading these few verses of songs you will see that God is a sure God. And he will be of assistance to you as soon as he sees you in need of help. At what time you go back to him? Be sure that you depend on him, let Jesus know your problems, he will make the way straight, let him know you are week and you need him always, and Jesus will assist you in every way he can. Keep Jesus in your heart, he cares for each and every one! The way of Salvation can only give you strength, when you put God first in all you or say. Allow him in, and believe in him always! He cares! After you really come to be acquainted with the Lord Jesus Christ as your personal savior from sin, and as you prayed constantly, and read the Bible! It becomes very filling. You don't even feel as if you need to eat the earthly meal. Jesus words can fill you up. It make's you feel like you always need to know more, and as you gain knowledge of how it is; you will always want to know more about our soon coming king. He is reel! The plan of salvation is a wonderful experience! As you come to know Jesus, you will understand the plan of salvation. You will love the way and experience in your heart the love he has for you! You will love the Lord Jesus Christ and will turn to him for ever thing you need. You will not be able to do any thing with out him in your lives. He becomes a part of your live! All you need to do is ask him for what you need and he will make a way. Its may seems hopeless some times, but just remember that he cares, and he die to save each and every one. Therefore there is nothing he will not execute for you. Jesus dies for us, because he love's us, and desires us to be saving in his father's kingdom. Thus he asks us to follow his words! We need to put him first in our lives. Then you can depend on him always. Jeremiah 11: 3 – 4 Tell's you that! The Lord said! Unto the inhabitants of Jerusalem saying cursed is the man that obeyed not the words of this covenant; which I commanded your fathers in the day that I brought them forth out of the land of Egypt, from the Iron furnace saying Obey my voice and do them according to all which I command you: So shall ye be my people, and I will be your God. You can see from the reading of God holy words, he is asking us to obey him and he will be our God. He loves us with on everlasting love! So we ought to love him as he first loves us. 1 Timothy 1: 1 -2 Said! Paul, an apostle of Jesus Christ by the commandment of God our Savior and Lord Jesus Christ, which is our hope unto Timothy my own son in the faith: Grace, mercy, and peace from God our father and Jesus Christ our Lord. Hebrews 5: 13, 14 Tell's you that! For ever one that useth milk is unskillful in the word of righteousness, for he is a babe. But strong meat belongeth on to them that are of age. As soon as we grow to be of age we should act as adult, and not as a babe, the good Lord ask us to be ready until he comes! And to be ready we have to grow to be on adult so we can be able to understand God's holy words. I have grown and understand God holy words and I would like to help others to know him also. Be strong and get off the milk and eat strong food as a result you can be on adult. Let your mind and understanding is stronger, as a result Jesus can use you. He can also use a child to lead you, but he want's you to be on adult, as a result he can use you to leads others to his kingdom. When you are week and feel as a child or even declining, just go to Jesus as you are and tell him your entire problem, he will here and answer you. Jesus cares for all his children and desires them to be present in his kingdom when he comes. There are times when I feel like there is no hope in life any more, and at the same time as I go to the Lord in prayer, even read his words, I could see that there is hope for us. Discerning the plan of salvation, and have to return to the world of sin is a heard thing to bear. Therefore put Jesus first in your heart! And he will be there for you constantly to guide you along the way! Jesus is love.

CHAPTER 69

THE SAVIOR IS AT YOUR DOOR! LET HIM IN! HE CARES FOR YOU ALWAYS!

At what time the savior is knocking at your door? You will know. He lives within your heart and you will feel his present worm within you. Just open and let him in, he loves you and care for you, no matter where you are or what you do, he is a helper and a deliver and advisory for you. Jesus is real! You only have to know him to be able to love him. Knowing God holy words is very important for you to know before accepting him into your lives. As you know him fully you will not desire to go back to the world of sin, unless it is a necessity. Jesus can help you to hold fast to him! Just put him first in your heart. There is always obstacle in our lives that we need to deal with. Some times you will feel as if you can not overcome through Jesus, -

However I can tell you that! You can overcome through Jesus! Just have faith in Jesus! He cares for us all. Prayer is the key to rely on Jesus! Lay all your trouble at the foot at the cross, and ask him to take the burden away. If I did not have faith in Jesus, I would be back in the world of sin. If you should come to the point where you see that you have to turn to the sinful world again? Just do not do any thing on your own, open your problem to Jesus, tell him what you need! He will here and answers prayer. Open your heart and let him in! Jesus wills here your cry, and he will lead you back onto the fold or righteousness, and help you to deal with all your problems! Jesus is the great deliverer. He cares for each and every one! Your life is in his hands, he just wants to help you, therefore he comes to you at the cross, and there he proves to you that he loves you with on everlasting love. The savior will comes to you when you need him or when you are in trouble. The song writer said! Just when you need him I will be there! Therefore never give up, or never turn away any one when you here the knock at your heart door. Your heart can feel at the same time as if you would like to open it to some one, and yet you harden your heart and say I just can't be bother! May be that's just the time the savior will be there trying to reach out to your hurting heart, and you shut him out. Jesus can open it for himself, however because he told us in his holy words that he want's us to have freedom of choice, that's why he knock to see if you will open to him as a willing heart. Love is Jesus! And if you have love in your heart, you will know Jesus is knocking at your heart door. Therefore you will know Jesus different from Satan. He will try to be like Jesus but he cannot have a sincere love, because he is not Jesus! Only Jesus is love. Satan can only try to show love, nevertheless when he don't have his way he goes back right into anger and hate. Jesus is love! No matter who you are or what you may have Jesus cares with on unchanging love. 1 John 4: 7 Tell's you that! Beloved, let us love one another: for love is of God, and every one that loveth is born of God, and knoweth God. 11 Corinthians 13: 11 Tell's you that! Finally, brethren, farewell be perfect, being of good comfort, be of one mind, live in peace; and the God of love and peace shall be with you. Therefore from reading these words from God holy words you can see that God is love! And he loves us for eternity. Read your Bible pray ever day, and keep Jesus in your heart and mind. He cares! Jesus need's to know if you really care and need him in your heart and mind, he could let you have him in your heart and mind with out giving you a chance to choose. However he desires you to have a chance to choose. Also Jesus desires you to know good things from bad things. Therefore he place before you Jesus and Satan! Satan will also try to do all things like Jesus! But! He will not be able to accomplish all things as Jesus does. For the reason that God did not give him that power to perform creating things like him since no one is as great as Jesus, he is the only one like his father. You have to know Jesus for your self to be able to make that choice. To know Jesus, go to him in prayer and ask him to open your mind to understanding his words. And read your Bible ever day. When you are going to read you're Bible, pray to Jesus and ask him to assist you to understand his words as you read them, Jesus words are life. You will love Jesus as you learn of him, and you will follow his words. As you come to know Jesus, you will understand the love and piece he can give you. You will never desire to leave his presents. The more you know about his mighty and powerful work, you will never wish for him to leave you Jesus is Love. 1 John 3: 18 Tell's you that! My little children let us love in words, nether in tongue; but in deed and in truth. Also Revelation 3: 20 Said! Behold, I stand at the door and knock; if any man here my voice, and open the door, I will come in to him, and will sup with him, and he with me. As you read these scriptures you will understand what I am speaking about in my writing. Jesus loves us and desires us to allow him into our lives. That's a privileges he granted unto us! He could let us perform what he asks us to accomplish with out letting us have a choice; however he is kind and loving to each and every one and desires us to have a choice, and to know him as our personal savior from sin. Jesus knows each and every one! That's why he dies on the cross for us, as a result that we may live. I have had experience of a bit of the cross! I know what it's like when Jesus said! It's finish! I have felt some of the pain, when you know why you are feeling the pain, and what it's for, God will give you the power to endured, and able to overcome it all. I have gone through it all, only the nail did not drive through my hands and feet. But I have felt it, that's the reason why I can tell you that Jesus love you all. I have come to know Jesus and love Jesus that's why I could endure, and over come. You can have Jesus in your heart also, and you can read his words and grew to love him, as a result that when trouble time comes your way, you will be able to overcome also. The cross is not on easy one to bear, but if you love Jesus you will not give up! You will keep holding on to his love and his words, and he will never failed you; Matthew 16: 24 Tell's you that! Then said Jesus unto his disciples, if any man will come after me, let him deny himself, and take up his cross and follow me. Mark 10: 27 Also Tell's you that! And Jesus looking upon them saith, with men it is impossible, but not with God: all things are possible. As you read these two scriptures you can see that God is able to do all things for us through his son Jesus Christ. Just put your trust in him and read his words and pray ever day, and he will here and answer you. You must have faith and trust in Jesus Christ our savior. He is Lord of all. Let him in your heart and mind.

CHAPTER 70

I AM HERE LORD! I OVERCOME THE STREAM AND THE VALLIES I COME FROM FOR AND NEAR.

Subsequent to you have accepted the Lord as your personal savior from sin! And you have cross over the stream and the valises, in the direction of coming to be acquainted with Jesus and say yes to him through baptism! You have to give him thanks for helping you to over come. I have to let you recognize that I have cross over them all; I only did not nail to the cross. When I have seen how much I have gone through, for and near difficult places, and yet Jesus have found me and prove himself to me. Any were I go, Jesus found me and help me to say yes to him. I have to give thanks by praying to Jesus, and reading his words. I also enlighten others about his wonderful love that he has given to me. I must advise others that Jesus has sought me and found me; therefore I have to praise his merciful name. I recognize Jesus has a special work for me to accomplish, as a result I open my mind ears and heart to him with love for him as a result he can use me in a mighty way. Jesus is love! We should first love him, and make an effort to gain knowledge of him; as a result he can find you and be of assistance to you. Proverbs 10: 12 Tell's you that! Hatred stirreth up strife's: but love covereth all sin. Ephesians 3; 19 Tell's you that! And to know the love of Christ, which passeth knowledge, that ye might be filled with all the fullness of God. As you read the scripture, you can see that Jesus is love and there is none other love that is greater than Jesus. Love will take you through all things. As a result of gaining knowledge of God great words, I say yes Lord I come to thee with open heart and mind.

CHAPTER 71

WHEN WE SEE THE SIGNS OF OUR LORD AND SAVIOR COMING, WE SHOULD BE CLOUSER DROWN TO HIM, NOT RUNING AWAY FROM HIM!

The pain of bearing the cross like Jesus did, is unbearable! Jesus is the only one who knows it all. I have to go with out a job to see the work that has to be done for Jesus Christ, the shame, the unthankful ness from others, who I help, and fail to give thanks to the work that help them, is very hurtful to me! I have to be humble and be peaceful as a result the Holy Spirit can inspire me constantly, as a result the Holy Spirit does not leave me, I cannot be angry! I have to seek other means to help my self while doing the will of God. It was so difficult for me, and no matter how difficult it may seem, I have to look after my children also. It's a pain I can not explain, my heart cry out to God in silence, I have to tell him all about my problems and wait for him to show me the right way to assist my self. I know Jesus will make a way for me no matter how long it may seem! I have no one to turn to, but Jesus, My children was away from me and my baby daughter was too small at the time to be of assistance to me! She was going through good and bad times with me; I have to depend on Jesus, who is the sure deliverer, he cares when no one cares, he can heal the pain and take away the grieve, and make the way straight. The sign we are seeing today are sing of the coming of our soon coming king. We should try to be closer drowning to him, as a result that when he comes we will not run away from his presence. I have to turn to him always! Jesus is making a way for me to overcome suffering, and be closer drowning to him. I give him thanks always! He is the only maker, if you trust him, believe in him and be honest, patient as you come to know the Lord, and savior Jesus Christ, you will overcome any obstacle. And if you desire to live for Jesus, you have to be sure that your work, and what ever you do or say, will be in his name honor and glory. As you ask for Jesus guidance he will have his angel with you always, to guide you always. When you are able to show love one for another, and then you will know that you are getting closer to the Lord and savior Jesus Christ. Romans 13: 8-10 Tell's you that! You should Owe no man any thing, but to love one another, for he that loveth another hath fulfilled the law, for this thou shalt not commit adultery, thou shalt not kill, thou shalt not steal, thou shalt not bear false witness, thou shalt not covet. And if there be any other commandment, it is briefly comprehended, in this saying, namely, thou shalt love thy neighbors as thyself. Love worketh no ill to his neighbors: therefore love is the fulfilling of the law. As you read these verves of scriptures you will see that love can leads and help you to care for others. Love is the key to know Jesus and follow his words. Read Jesus words, and does them by helping others to be acquainted with Jesus, and you will not run away from him when he burst the cloud of heaven with his ark angels. You will run to him, because you were ready for his coming. Jesus cares for us all he loves us first, as a result we can follow his foot step by loving him back. Jesus is love.

CHAPTER 72

WHEN A SAVIOR KNOCKS AT YOUR DOOR, DO YOU KNOW IT'S THE SAVIOR?

Sometimes we would see a person and may be he or she not looking up to your standard, and we turn him or her away, not knowing that could be on angel sent from God to let you know that Jesus cares for you and love you. We as a child of God should endeavor to love with God love, as a result when we see others knock at your door you will be able to pay attention for a moment. I have seeing people hurting me, by doing me wrong, and yet I love them, because Jesus said forgive them for they know not what they have done. I even sometime ask myself why I have to be that approach. I come to realized that I am a child of God. I did not have any controlled over myself, I just have to love when Jesus say love others. I know it was for a good cause. A prophet or a prophetess is one who has to go through a lot of trial and tribulation to be acquainted with Jesus. and to know that is Jesus leading them. I could not even cry any more, I have to just open my heart to Jesus and ask him to lead me constantly. I can not do any thing with out Jesus! One thing I really know, I love him and have him in my heart, I think that is the only way he could open my eyes to his words and his work. I have been face with so many different works; I have to have God's help to lead the way. I have to have a clear mind and strength to do his will. He always sends his help in many different ways. I have gone through stage where I was push to be dirty, studied, lazy, and with out friends. And Jesus took me out of all those problems through his messenger. I meet him through my child when I was taking her to school. I have been crushed like Daniel in the Lion den, God take me out of danger. They have laid me down to die, and I have seen God raised me up with more strength. When all these things were happening to me I did not know why it was happening therefore, all I used to do is cry and pray to God, I was like a child again. I could remember asking friends to help me, and none could help me. I came to prove Jesus as a loving savior who can save you from all danger. And I love him better ever day, therefore I would like each and every one to try and follow his words carefully, because his words is based on love. I could remember there was one person I have seen hurting me, I can tell you this! The good Lord woke me up one morning and tell me I should go and tell him what he was doing to me, and he should stop. That person was my brother who I care for a lot and respected. I got up and start signing, and I prayed, I went into my car and drove at about 60-65 miles per hour to get to his house. I woke him up and I told him I see that he was hurting me! He say it was not true, I turn to him and told him, if it was not true he must search himself and see if you have done any wrong, and go to God and ask for forgiveness. I leave and go back to my home, later in the after noon he came to my home. I was told not to open the door and let him in. And I did as I was told. I could not deal with him at that time. God said! He have to speak to my brother, I could not do it on my own. After that had happened I come to realized that I am a child of God. I did not have any controlled over myself, I just have to love the Lord as he say love. Love is the key to heaven; we should always love one another. As Jesus ask us to do. I accepted the Lord as my personal savior from sin, all over again, I was baptized when I was twelve years of age, I got married at the age of seventeen and have five children after the marriage. Life began to get very difficult for me; therefore I start to travel out to different countries to see if I could get life in a better way and help my husband take care of the children. It was too difficult for me after I reside in the U.S.A and my own, and was working too heard. I got sick! I was working, going to school, and I realized the good Lord was training me in the direction of performing his work, at the same time. I become so nervous and I had to quit one of my jobs and keep one. As I start to learn that Jesus was the answer to all my problems I accept Jesus as my personal savior from sin. And I promise that I would never turn away from Jesus present again. As a result the good Lord keeps me going through life with out any sickness. I always ask Jesus in my prayer to take care of my children, me and my husband. Also others! I got divorce and my husband remarried again, because I was absent for a long period of time I did not have any control over me staying away. It was like my hands and feet were tied, I could just make small amount of money, and I could not go and see my children, my life become so difficult at times. I always cried and prayed to the good Lord to help me! I taught I could not over come the difficulties. I never give up, then I got the strength to stop crying and try to salve problems I just try to find a way at all times to over come, and Jesus constantly show me the way. He will never fail me. Hebrew 11: 33 said! Through faith you can over come any problem, through faith subdued kingdom, wrought righteousness, obtained promises, and stopped the mouth of lions. As a result we should put our trust in the Lord and savior Jesus Christ. He is able to do all things. Mark 11: 26 Tell's you that! We should have faith, and believe in God. And Jesus answering unto them, Have faith in God! For verily I say unto you, that whosoever shall say unto this mountain, be thou removed and be thou cost into the sea, and shall not doubt in his heart, but shall believe that those thing which he saith shall come to pass; he shall have whatsoever he saith. Therefore I say unto you, what things so ever ye desire, when ye pray, believe that ye receive them and ye shall have them. And when ye stand praying forgive, if ye have aught against any that your father also which is in heaven for give your trespasses. As you read these verses of scriptures you will see that praying and believing and having faith, they all work together! To be able to have that kind of faith we have to first love Jesus and are able to believe that he can help you to achieve any thing you ask him to allow you to accomplish. Jesus knows us, and he knows what we need! All he want's us to accomplish is to put our trust in him always. Do his will, obey his words. Colossians 2: 7 Tell's you that! You should root and build up in him, and established in the faith, as ye have been taught, abounding therein with thanksgiving. If we can only built our self in having faith in God, and perform his will, he is able to assist us in accomplish all things. As we ask he will grant it unto us. Jesus said! We should not give up, no matter how hopeless and difficult life may seem. That's why we need faith to have over coming power. After you read these words from the scriptures and see how great and marvelous it is when you have faith in God. You should prayed every day to the good Lord and ask him to assist you to have faith in him and believe in his words. When the savior knock at your door! God may be sending you assistance, let him in and received it. Jesus cares for us all. Jesus can allow you to have the greatest faith that can move mountain and brake down barriers! Jesus cares for us all and want's us to believe in him always.

CHAPTER 73

JESUS SAVE!

A s soon as Jesus save you from all unrighteousness' you will know that is he, who save you! Your love for Jesus will become stronger. You will always wishes to serve him, no matter how difficult life may appear. Jesus is the savior of which our life depends on. He will never hurt you; he love's you with on everlasting love, that's why he dies on the cross for you and for me. When you have faith in Jesus and believe in him you will allow him in your heart and mind and he will recognize that you love him back with on everlasting love. Romans 10: 13, 17 Tell's you that! For whosoever shall call upon the name of the Lord shall be saved. Jesus also said! So then faith cometh by hearing, and hearing by the word of God. Genesis 14: 10 Said! And he believed in the Lord, and counted it to him for righteousness'. Romans 13: 10, Tell's you that! Love worketh no ill to his neighbor: Therefore love is the fulfilling of the law. Jesus saves through his love for us. Love is the law of God, and the fulfillment of the word of God! We have to follow his words as a result he can save us. At what time you come to be acquainted with the Lord and savior Jesus Christ, as your personal savior from sin through baptism and saying yes to Jesus! Then you will feel a wonderful joy bubbling in your heart that you would like to be with you for ever. That's how you will distinguish that the savior is with you. The savior is love! At what time you engrave Jesus in your heart; there will be joy in your heart always. The Bible said! The present of the Lord will not be with you always! But if you love him his Holy Spirit will be with you always, if you let him in your heart. Revelation 11: 1-3 Tell's you that! And there was given me a reed likes unto a rod: and the angel stood, saying rise and measure the temple of God and the altar, and them that worship therein. But the court which is without the temple leaves out, and measures it not: for it is given unto the Gentiles: And the Holy city shall they tread under foot frothy and two months. And I will give power unto my two witnesses, and they shall prophesy a thousand two hundreds and three score days, clothed in sock cloth. These are the two olive trees, and the two candlesticks standing before the God of the earth. Romans 10: 8-10, Tell's you that! But what saith? The word is nigh thee, even in thy mouth, and in the heart: that is the word of faith, which we preach; that if thou shalt confess which thy mouth the Lord Jesus, and shall believe in thine heart that God hath raised him from the dead, thou shalt be saved. "According to the reading of this scripture," you can see that God will give you all the measure of his angels to guide you as you acknowledge him, and love him with on everlasting love. As you believe that God raised Jesus from the grave, he will save you! Jesus said! When one sinner is saved in his kingdom he rejoices. Jesus will save all who trust and believe in his words. He do not forsake any one of his creatures, Jesus would like all to come to be acquainted with him, and love him and follow his words. When you come to be acquainted with him and accept his love for you, and be baptizing through his holy words, then you will know you are entering into his kingdom. Jesus is a savior! He cares for us all. Jesus knows our taught and our minds when we think and how we think. Jesus know who need him in their hearts and who don't need him in their hearts, he desires us each and every one to be saved in his kingdom. Jesus could let us all serve him with out us desire to or not! But he gave us a mind to have a free choice; as a result we can make choices of our own. He wants us to be responsible for our own souls! We have to know right from wrong, for us to be able to make the right choices. We ought to love him as he first loves us! That's why he says we must follow his foot step. He walk the part way that was painfully for us, as a result we could follow his words and be saved in his father's kingdom. We as children of God should read his holy words and pray always for his guiding angels to leads us along the way into righteousness. It's very important for the saving of our souls! At what time you have the savior with you, your days will be brighter, your needs will be supply, and your love for others will be stronger. The saver will give you the understanding you need to do all the things that is right in the sight of God. We should put him first in our lives, and as we follow his words carefully, he will open doors that could not be open to you before, he will make a way were there is no way. Jesus is the savior that cares for us all and he dies so that we may have the opportrinty of living when he comes to judge his people. So why not serve him? as a result that we may be able to enter into his father kingdom when he comes to redeem us again, St. John 3: 3, 5 Tell's you that! Jesus answer and said unto him, verily, verily, I say unto thee, except a man is born again, he cannot see the kingdom God! Verse 5 said! Jesus answered, verily, verily; I say unto thee, except a man is born of water and of the Spirit, he cannot enter into the kingdom of God. Jesus walks that part way, as a result he could do his father will. Therefore he is asking us to follow his foot step. Jesus was baptize by Peter, because he love his father and want to do as he ask him to do. Jesus has to depart from his disciples, just to be in peace with his father. To do is father's will was very important to him! Jesus knows through his father's teaching that he had to be in peace with the Holy Spirit sometimes! When he prayed by himself with the Holy angels he knows that he is communicating with is father in peace. And he will be able to be familiar with going about is father business, and how he desires to performed. Philemon 1: 5-16 Tell's you that! Hearing of thy love and faith, which thou hast toward the Lord Jesus and toward all saints, that the communication of the faith may become effectual by the acknowledging of every good thing which is in you in Christ Jesus, for we have great joy and consolation in thy love, because the bowels of saints are refreshed by thee, brother. Wherefore, though I might be much bold in Christ to enjoin thee that which is convenient, yet for love's sake I rather beseech thee, being such a one as Paul the aged, and now also a prisoner of Jesus Christ. I beseech thee for my son O-nes-i-mus, whom I have begotten in my bonds, which in time past was to thee unprofitable, but now profitable to thee and to me. Whom I have sent again: thou therefore receive him that is mine own bowels; Whom I would have retained with me, that in thy stead he might have ministered unto me in the bonds of the gospel: But without thy mind would I do nothing; that thy benefit should not be as it were of necessity, but willingly. For perhaps he therefore departed for a season, that thou shouldest receive him for ever. Not now as a servant, but above a servant, a brother beloved, specially to me but how much more unto thee both in the flesh, and in the Lord. Therefore from the reading of these holy words you can see that when you depart from brethren, family and friends, it's for a good reason, to be able to communicate with the Lord Jesus in secrete. It's very important to go to the Lord when you need him. You will gather strength from the holy angels, as a result you will be able to tell your brethren and friends more about Jesus love and his wonderful plan he has in store for us, in boldness from God. God love for us is great and marvelous; we have to be in peace, as a result we can be able to be acquainted with Jesus, different from the plan of Satan! God is love! Therefore we of to be closure drown to him each day in prayer, as a result we can be acquainted with him. Jesus love is always, and he cares for each and every one of us. Let us put him first in our daily lives. Jesus walks among sinner as a result he can save them! Jesus is holy son of God who dies on the cross for us; as a result we can be saving in his kingdom. Jesus loves sinner, no matter how hopeless their sins may be. Therefore when you accept Christ as your personal savior from sin, you have to walk among sinners; as a result you may be able to win their souls for the kingdom of God. Christian should not be separated from sinners! You should always take them as your friends, accordingly you can tell them about Jesus love for them. Jesus knows our taught and our minds. He knows we would separate our self from sinners after we accept him, that's why he first eat and drink with sinners as a result we can follow his foot step, and to let us understand what it means to him to unite with sinners. The people that are in sin! Need Christian to be of assistance to them in the direction of knowing the Lord and savior Jesus Christ. Jesus said! As you be on familiar terms with Jesus, you should tell others about him and how he cares for them. Luke 15: 1-10 Tell's you that! Then drew near unto him all the publicans and sinners for to here him and the Pharisees and scribes murmured saying, this man receiveth sinners and eateth with them. And he spake this parable unto them saying! What man of you having an hundred sheep, if he lost one of them, doth not leave the ninety and nine in the wilderness, and go after that which is lost, until he finds it? And when he hath found it, he layeth it on his shoulders, rejoicing. And when he cometh home, he calleth together his friends and neighbors, saying unto them, rejoice with me, for I have found my sheep which was lost. I say unto you that likewise joy shall be in heaven over one sinner that repenteth, more than over nineth and nine just persons, which need no repentance. What woman having ten pieces of silver, if she lose one piece, doth, not light a candle, and sweep the house and seek diligently till she find it. And when she hath found it she calleth her friends and her neighbors together, saying rejoice with me for I have found the piece which I had lost. Likewise I say unto you there is joy in the presence of the angels of God over one sinner that repenteth. As you read this scripture you can see that Jesus walks among sinners because he loves them, and want's to save them. The person that is sick needs a doctor! But when the person is not sick he or she is not in need of a doctor. Therefore you can see again, sinners need the assistance of a Christian. Let us love one another as a result we can be like Jesus. He cares for us all! To save a sinner you must unite with them, unity is strength. Jesus loves unite! Jesus said! Where two or three is gathering in my name they are blessed. When you as a Christian, is uniting with sinners you must know the work of God, and how to speak to others, and what you can accomplish with sinners. First you be acquainted with using the words from God holy Bible to lead them. They need your assistance, therefore you must be able to lead through Jesus holy words, if you should give in to any of their wrong doing, and they will lead you into unrighteousness. Therefore be strong in the Lord, and endeavor to be Holy as Jesus asks us to be Holy as he does before you can help a sinner. Colossians 3: 12-17 Tell's you that! You should put therefore, as the elect of God, holy and beloved, bowels of mercies, kindness, humbleness of mind, meekness, longsuffering; forbearing one another, and forgiving one another, if any man have a quarrel against any: even as Christ forgive you, so also do ye. And above all these things put on charity, which is the bind of perfectness. And let the peace of God rule in your heart to which also ye are called in one body; and be ye thankful. Let the word of Christ dwell in you richly in all wisdom; teaching and admonishing one another in psalm and hymns and spiritual songs, singing with grace in your heart to the Lord. And whatsoever ye do in word or deed, do all in the name of the Lord Jesus, giving thanks to God and the father by him. Therefore from the holy words from the Bible, you can see as a result of you being strong in the Lord words you will be able to save sinners into God kingdom.

CHAPTER 74

WHEN WE SEE THE SIGNS OF OUR LORD AND SAVIOR, WE SHOULD BE CLOUSER DROWNING TO HIM!

Jesus speaks about all the signs that we are seeing today's world, in his words Jesus always asking us to follow his words by doing his will. He tells each and every one we need to follow his words as a result when difficulty come our way, we will be able to overcome through his promises. The signs that we are seeing today, are signs that only a number of people can be able to overcome. They are painful; they hurt so bad only the good Lord can help any one to overcome. The Bible speak of wars and roomers of war, these are the signs we are living in the midst of today. We have to have Jesus in our hearts to be acquainted with him. As we are familiar with him we should assist others to know him, the more you do for Jesus, the more he will make a way for you. No matter how difficult your problems are. Go to Jesus in prayer, with a sincere heart, he will be of assistance to you in the direction of loving him and serve him. It's not on easy obsession to accomplish even after you are acquainted with Jesus, and accept him, and trying to serve him. You have to have faith through God, in other to be acquainted with him and serve him, it's not easy! But you have to have faith through God, to discern and serve Jesus. After being in Church! There is where you will find Satan testing your faith. You can only have through faith through strong faith in God. God can break all barriers down, just trust him, and always have him in your hearts. Sometimes it will seem very heard that you would feel like giving up. Don't ever give up, he will never leave you are forsake you. You have to believe in his holy words. Sometimes you will even feel like leaving, because of the experience you have seen in the church, doesn't ever leave! Strive to used your own ideas and assist in any way you can, visit others churches, pray ever day ask the good Lord to show you the way to be of assistance to his people. Jesus need to use you taught and mind to help his people! God give the Posters knowledge to train his people, through sending them to collage as a result they can know more about his words. God also have other ways of training his servants who he identifies as his prophets and prophetess, which he trained through his power, with his holy angels, which is greater in various ways. Sometimes that person can be your father or mother or even a stranger! Jesus desires us to discern him and serve him. Therefore we have to give careful attention to those servants; as a result we can recognize him! He is wonderful when we come to know him; you will love him and wants to serve him always. God is love! He is sure, he is true, only trust him and believe in his words. Jesus is always willing to be of assistance to you, he is very patient, and you solitary have to learn to be familiar with him. Pray always and he will answer your prayers. Jesus is coming very soon, and we should try to be honest. There was on accident took place in the U.S.A. and thousand of people were trap in that accident and were killed! Thousand of people did not have the opportunity to call on the Lord Jesus Christ, it happen so fast only a few people were able to escape. Tears flow all over the world for lost souls. There were hundreds of people also in airplanes that were also killed! The plain crashed into the world trade tower was not on accident, that was wicked people taking others people lives, also the people in the plain die because of wicked people. All those people die in one day; those are signs of God coming. Jesus said these things will happen in a twinkling of on eye. This world can be lost in a moment, the Bible speak truth. All those that were already accept Jesus can be saved when Jesus comes! Let us try to find him through his holy words and serve him, and be ready to enter into his kingdom. Take these signs as a signal and be closer drowning to the Lord Jesus Christ. He is near and we should be ready! As a result when these things happen, our spirit will be in the arms of Jesus. Those people die doing what the Lord said we should do, Jesus said! By the sweet of your brow you shall live and eat! They were working for an honest living, while the wicked ones were planning to take their lives. May the good have mercy on their souls when he comes! Some may be ready some may never heard of the Lord Jesus Christ. The Lord desires us to be ready! That's why he gave us the Bible as a guide as a result we can follow him. These things must come to pass before Jesus comes to redeem us to be in heaven with him! The ones that were pass away and were ready to meet their savior, are just sleeping, they will rise again and be joyful when Jesus comes. Those that did not be acquainted with the Lord will rise again only to here depart from me because I know you not. They were not ready to meet their savior. God said! He gave his only begotten son to die for us; as a result we will be able to live again. If we follow his words we will live again after death. When we go out to work are to perform our own business, we need not to worry, for the reason that we are in the hands of our savior any were we are. God will take care of us weather we die are alive. We all mourned for the people friends and family! But we can not be of assistance to any one after they are gone on before. Let us now unite together as our President ask all people to go before the Lord in prayer to pray for the people that was gone, and those that were left to mourned. Let us be ready for our Lord. The words of Jesus must fulfill subsequently for us to be able to overcome with joy, we must be ready for our Lord's return. To be ready we must believe in the words of Jesus, we must study them and exercise them in our daily lives. Revelation 1:1-3 Tell's you that! The Revelation of Jesus Christ, which God gave unto his servants, things which must shortly come to pass, and he sent and signified it by his angels unto his servant John. Who bare record of the word of God, and of the Testimony of Jesus Christ, and of all things that he saw. Blessed is he that readeth, and they that here the words of this prophecy, and keep those things which are written there in. For the time is at hand. Therefore you can see from the words of God we all need to be ready. Jesus is the only answer to all our needs. We all need to keep Jesus always in our hearts. To be acquainted with our Lord and savior Jesus Christ, it can be a very difficult experience, but we should never give up. Pray always and the good Lord will give you strength to endure. Some times the experience can be very hurting, but you must always put love first in your heart! As soon as you have love, you will find Jesus, because Jesus is love. And Jesus will assist you to over come any obstacle in your lives. To know Jesus as your personal savior from sin, you will always face with trials and tribulation. By using all the testing and be strong in God. Jesus loves you always and desires each and every one to be saved in his kingdom. I have on experience on the 11-05-01 there was on hurricane treat on the news, and there was rain all over the Land of south Florida, I should have gone to work on that morning, I call my patient, and told her I did not sure I would be able to come to work that morning, because of the weather. I was told by the Holy Spirit to stay in doors that day, I went to the door several times checking on the looks of the weather. I was thinking about my patient more than the words of the Holy Spirit. I decided after the rain stop for a moment I would go to work. I went out and took the bus, I went on the first bus feeling a little scared, after taking the second bus, I begun to feel more scared, I travel for a little while on the bus, as I got close to the air port, the bus was going over a bridge, the bus come to a stop on the bridge and the bus was lean on the left side. I got so scared; I could not sit down on any seat on the bus. I said to my self I will not go any forder on this bus; I will come off at the next bus stop. I did not worry any more about the patient, I remember Jonah on the boat, when the Lord gave him a massage to tell the people of Nineveh, and he run away on the boat. Therefore I said to my self I must obey the Holy Spirit. I got off the bus and waited for the next return bus to take me home. I waited for a long time before I got the returned bus. As soon as I got the bus I went back home. My patient calls me to find out where I was, and if I was coming to work. I told her what happened and tell her I will come the next morning. At what time you come to know the Lord, you have to follow his angels, they are always with you. Jesus had to use any means to get me to do his will! That is why the bus had to stop at that point on the bridge. Jesus is reel; we should all try to be acquainted with Jesus! Jonah 1: 1- 17 Tell's you about the story of Jonah, when Jesus gave him a massage to go to Nineveh to tell the people about their wickedness. He disobeyed and they cost him in the sea. Jonah was scared to perform God will! Therefore he tried to run away on a boat, to another city. God stop him along the way through a storm, all he could said to the people when they go to him while he was sleeping on the bout, the people woke him up and ask him what they should do? His reply was, the storm was through him, and they should through him over board and the wind and rain would stop. They did as they were told, and the wind and rain stop. As I was sitting there on the bus that was all that came to my mind, also I heard a still voice said to me get off and walk. I said to myself I can not walk from where I was back to home! I said to my self again, I will get off this bus at the next stop, so I did and went back home. As the rain continued I could not say a word. I just keep watching the rain and was too scared even too prayed at that time. I just hold my heart closure to God; just to let him recognize that I know what he desires me to execute. I distinguish right there and then that he is reel again. I have proven him in many different ways. I know the devil is fighting like a lion to stop me from doing the will of God! But I know I will not do what the devil wishes in any way. I will execute the will of God in any way I can, to prove to the devil that he is a lire. Therefore that is why I write this chapter to let others recognize that God is reel. Jesus said we should tell others of his love for us and of his words, as we understand it. Therefore this is one of my ways of helping others to know Jesus. Jesus loves us and would like us to be saved in his father's kingdom when he comes. We should read the Bible and pray constantly, and he will open your eyes and mind so you will understand his will. To discern the Lord as your personal savior from sin, you must first love him. He may put you through difficult times as testing of your faith, just to see if you really love him and wants to serve him. When these things happen, never give up; hold more to the Lord through prayer and fasting. And he will give you strength to over come all things. The words of the Bible are life and love! Keep them in your heart as you learn of them! Jesus bear the cross alone, because he loves us and wants us to be save in his father's kingdom, he will not let you die on the cross because he suffer and die for us, so we may obey his words. Follow him by doing his words! He loves us with on everlasting love. Jesus love for us is the reason he die for us on the curial cross! He did not have to go through suffering and pain on the cross for us, his father could stop all that was happening to him, but he did not do so, because he want all human beans to be saved. Jesus ask us to follow his foot step by reading his words and doing them, so that when he and his father and his angels return on earth we will be ready and able to enter into his father's kingdom. He rise from the grave to show us that he lives again, so we will be able to live also. In the Seven-day-Adventist Church, we as members of the Church have to exercise what we speak, so we can bring others to see the truth. Jesus gives us the Ten-Commandments so we can follower his words carefully! We should not exercise one part of God Laws, and do not do the other. In the Commandments is two very important parts of the Ten-Commandments that we need to pay careful attention to! We should try to do what it said! Honor your mother and father, that your days may be long, upon the land which the Lord thy God gives thee. It's very easy for human bean to make a mistake, the reason I say we as members should pay careful attention! We always have testing of our faith, the parent may say something to his or her child, which may not sound good, and we exercise the wrong behavior, we should always try to show love in every way, so that they may not see things the wrong way. We have to learn to help them in what every way we can, and still love them always. Remember what the Bible says, and you will get the strength to do what so every have to be done. The second one is covet! We should not try to want what others have when you can't have it; sometimes we sin in simple ways of which we do not even realized. We may see a friend with some thing that we think we should have, that can be a sin in God's eyes. Some times we even try to get it by fighting for it it's a sin also, Satan will leads you because of your taught, those taught gives Satan strength to over come you. He will put it in your mind even more that you are the better person for those things, go and get it, as soon as that happen God will have to let him take you over because he is not a God that fights for any thing. God let you have your own choice so you can chouse him or Satan. So please brothers and sisters and friends, do not let him in, keep God in your heart with what you need, not what you want, God love you all and he will let you have what you need through his love. Jesus needs to know that you love him and he can help you through bad times and good times. Jesus knows we sometimes said, we love him and yet we do not keep his Commandments. To prove to Jesus that we love him, we have to serve him with all our hearts. Some times it's seems like a much heard thing to do, but you have to have faith in his promises! Making a decision to serve Jesus is a very important thing to do. We can only make that decision through Jesus love. Jesus want's us to ask him to help us, he wants us to have a willing heart, and need to know him with a willing heart. We need to ask him for help through prayer and through studying his words. To be a University trained student from God is not very easy. It takes me 11 years to be trained for Jesus work. You have to know Jesus different from Satan to be able to manage Jesus work. Jesus ways is not easy, but it is sure and pure. I cried many days, but it comes to the end to know it was really the son of God; it was really sweeter than the days before. I love Jesus better ever day! There are no more scarier tares, only tears of joy now. God said! You should have faith in him so that when the gun man faces you he or she will not be able to hurt you. They will want to know who you are. Jesus is a saver! We should seek him now. Knowing Jesus before its too late is very important. There was an accident in Jamaica, with take the lives of several men, and have several injured and was sent to the hospital for several months. There was one man who was injured very badly, and has to be in the hospital for several months, this man live with his girl friend for several years and have seven children with her. After the accident they wanted was to give him money for his family, but he could not get any for his wife because he was not married to her. On his dying bed he had to married to his girl friend so he could get the money for her and the children. Marring to your girl friend as you live together and having children is very important, just like saying yes to Jesus through baptism is very important. You have to be ready for Jesus as he asks you to, just as we have to keep the laws of our lands so we can be ready for all the right reasons. Marriage and baptism is very important we should try to follow those vows because they are from God's Holy words! I would like every one to have Jesus love, so that when we see love we can know it and follow. Jesus is love, and he can save you, trust in his words.

CHAPTER 75

WHEN A CHILD IS BORN FROM HER MOTHER'S WHOME!

A child is as a helpless little thing, who need attention at all times. The child has to be trained to eat from the mother's breast or a little bottle of milk. The child has to be trained as it grew how to feed him or her self, also how to take a bath. As the child grew he or she has to go to school to be trained how to read and write so they can manage as they become on adult. The time a child take to be trained from a baby to on adult is about 20- to 25 years of age or even more, to be able to work and take care of him or her self. I am telling you about this newborn child because I like to tell you that when Jesus is training his servant to do his work, he or she become a like a new born baby and has to be trained for a period of years until he or she is able to know Satan different from God Holy Spirit, so you will be able to do God work, and tell other that Jesus lives. When you began to train! Trial and tribulation just began, so you have to be strong in the Lord and never give up on his training. Jesus will understand and know that you are not yet trained; these things have to happen so you can know Jesus different from Satan, and understand his Holy Spirit. As soon as you are trained, and ready to work for Jesus you will know as he put you to work for him. When you start to work for Jesus you will know you cannot do things you used to do any more. Jesus will have a strong power over you and you must know that it is the Holy Spirit working with you. Jesus is patient and he will wait until you are strong and able to work for him. To know Jesus! And what he stand for is very important! Jesus need you to know him so you can serve him and brings others to him. 1 Corinthians 2: 10-14 Said! But God hath revealed them unto us by his Spirit: for the Spirit searcheth all things. Yea, the deep things of God for what man knoweth the things of a man, save the Spirit of man which is in him? Even so the things of God knoweth no man but the Spirit of God. Now we have received, not the Spirit of the world, but the Spirit which is of God; that we might know the things that we freely given to us through God. Which things also we speak not in the words which man's wisdom teacheth; but which the Holy Ghost teacheth; comparing Spiritual things with Spiritual. But the natural man receiveth not the things of the Spirit of God: for they are foolishness unto him: nether can he know them because they are spiritually discerned. Also Isaiah 28:9 Tell's you that! When shall he teach knowledge? And whom shall he make to understand doctrine, them that are weaned from the milk, and drown from the breasts. As you read these scriptures you can see! To be trained is very important to God. God needs you to know him with understanding. When a child is born with growing up, you have to show that child love, also you have to train the child with understanding, so that child will be able to work and take care of him or her self when they become an adult. You also have to help that child with what ever needs he or she wants in life until he or she be of age to take care of them selves. The same needs may apply to God servants, because they become like a child again some times. The servants of God may be able to work for them selves, but if they need help in any way, they should receive it. Jesus is love, longsuffering, and over coming power! When you come to actually know Jesus as your personal savior from sin, you will never want to leave his present or turn away from his words. You will constantly like to praise Jesus and love him. Jesus cares for us all! Try and served him always. To know him you may have to suffer for a while, but never give up, he can help you to over come all obstacles. And have you rejoicing in his mighty and powerful name. The Lord of heaven and earth is mighty and powerful in his work! We all need to learn of him and what he expects of us. Just put your heart and mind into his words, and you can learn from them! They are true and powerful words. They are life. The Lord of heaven and earth just want to know you love him, and accept his calling, when he calls you. You will never run away from him again, because he will find you were ever you are. He cares for you that why he will never leave you until you know him, and want to serve him always. As you know Jesus you will always running to him through his words and prayer. 11 Corinthians 8: 4 Tell's you that! Praying us with much entreaty that we would receive the gift, and take upon us the fellowship of the ministering to the saints, verse 9 also said! For ye know the grace of our Lord Jesus Christ, that through he was rich, yet for your sake he become poor, that ye through his poverty might be rich, verse 21 also said! Proving for honest things not only in the sight of the Lord, but also in the sight of men, when you acknowledge God grace and his loving mercy, then you will want to minister to others. Jesus cares and wants us to know him always, try Jesus now. To know Jesus may cause you pain and suffering, but as you know him it will bring you joy always. When you have a parent that will help you in your young age you should always be obedient to them in ever way. Jesus gives them to us as a guide line, so he or she can train you from early age. If you do not give your parents careful attention when they speak to you, you will have no problem. Jesus used angels to train you! There is different ways of training a child, if you disobey parent's order which may seem heard to you, and then he will have no other choice but to punish you. Punishments can come in many different ways Try to obey your parents it may be easer to obey God's calling. Don't let it be punishment! I may be painful and long suffering. Jesus as gone through long suffering and he can use it to let you know him. Jesus cares! A parent is a very important part in a child life. Some parent try in every way to train their child or children through God's holy words. When you put them in the hands of the Lord, he will make a way for them at all times. They need Jesus to take them through life. Parents you are their first help, to eternal life. They depend on you from the time they were conceiving until the time child reach of age to take care of them self. Please do your part through God, so you can receive your blessing. It's very important! God has special servants who can help us to know him. A minister is a very important person! When God help a person to know him so he or she can help others to come to him, it's very important. We should always train our children to pay careful attention to him. Jesus said! We should put him first, but some times it really do not happen that way, because when we are very young and in the wrong environment, we tens to pay attention to the things of the world, until Jesus get ready and say we must get ready now. Jesus know our taughts and our thinking, he know if we need him, so if we even go astray through others, he can take us from any were we are. So all I am asking is for you to give Jesus a part in your heart and your mind. Jesus knows that we are week in mind and heart. But if you ask him he will help you to be strong, and overcome any difficulty you may faces. 11 Timothy 1: 12-17 Tell's you that! For which cause I also suffer these things; nevertheless I am not ashamed: for I know whom I have believed, and am persuaded that he is able to keep that which I have committed unto him against that day. You must hold fast the form of sound words which thou hast heard of me, in faith and love which is in Christ Jesus. That good thing which was committed unto thee keeps by the Holy

Ghost which dwelleth in us. Verse 17 Tell's you that! But when he was in Rome, he sought me out very diligently, and found me. And when he found you and you overcome, you must serve him. Revelation 3:5 Tell's you! He that overcometh, the same shall be clothed in white raiment: and I will not blot out his name out of the book of life. But I will confess his name before my father and before his angels. Be ye ready for our Lord and savior will soon to come. Train our new born at on early age so that they will be ready also. Jesus loves us all.

Printed in the United States
By Bookmasters